BEYOND
THE BULL

BEYOND
THE BULL

TAKING
STOCK MARKET WISDOM
TO THE NEXT LEVEL

KEN NORQUAY

Published by
BPS Books
Toronto, Canada
www.bpsbooks.net
A division of Bastian Publishing Services Ltd.

ISBN 978-0-9809231-8-6

Cataloguing in Publication Data available from Library and Archives Canada.

Cover design, text design, and typesetting:
Tannice Goddard, Soul Oasis Networking

To my Teacher and Spiritual Guide, Mervyn Brady
FEBRUARY 11, 1948–APRIL 27, 2006

Contents

Preface

DO YOU EVER WONDER about the stock market? Not as in, "I wonder why I lost money ..." Or as in, "I wonder how to make money ..." But just wonder?

A famous study shows that randomly selected portfolios of stocks consistently outperform portfolios of stocks picked by the industry's top analysts. How can this be?

Other studies have shown that 80% of all mutual funds under-perform stock market averages. How can this be?

On the surface, these facts seem to defy logic.

When I was a rookie stockbroker with Merrill Lynch, back in 1975, I too wondered. About halfway through my long career in the investing business, I took up a new hobby: I started to study mysticism and ancient philosophy.

I learned that Buddhists believe this world is an illusion; the real world is hidden. Could this be true of the stock market?

The shamanic traditions of the indigenous peoples of Central and South America also talk about two worlds: the tonal world and the nagual world: the concrete world of everyday life and the mysterious world of the fifth dimension. Is there a hidden dimension to the financial world?

Judaism and Christianity talk about a great battle between the forces of good and evil. Writers and moviemakers have created *The Matrix*, *The Lord of the Rings*, and *The Chronicles of Narnia* to illustrate this mysterious battle. Is the stock market further evidence of this struggle?

The ancient Greeks believed that the gods of Mount Olympus were like mysterious chess masters with humans as their innocent chess pieces, to be manipulated mercilessly. Are our lives as stock market investors manipulated by divine forces?

Martial arts philosophy views the world as a struggle for survival. There are the weak and the strong. There are winners and losers. Could this be true of the stock market, too?

The experience of making and losing money in the stock market has made me a practical man. But my study of ancient wisdom has added context to that experience. Yes, there is a hidden component to the market. Yes, there are two worlds. Yes, the stock market is a battle. Yes, much of what happens seems beyond our control. Yes, we must fight to survive. Practicality requires us to know the truth about investing. This book is my best take on that truth. It represents a major move beyond the bull — the salesmanship, the advertising, the facile advice of financial advisors, as well as investors' own emotional and irrational fears and motivations — to a higher wisdom about the stock market.

Practical people often say, "You can't take it with you." The wisest of our forefathers disagreed. They would have us believe there *is* something we can take from this world to the next.

I have written this book in hopes that my readers will take something valuable with them. And leave something valuable behind.

Ken Norquay
Financial Philosopher

Introduction

THE TYGER

Tyger, Tyger, burning bright
In the forests of the night,
What immortal hand or eye
Could frame thy fearful symmetry?

In what distant deeps or skies
Burnt the fire of thine eyes?
On what wings dare he aspire?
What the hand dare seize the fire?

And what shoulder and what art
Could twist the sinews of thy heart?
And when thy heart began to beat,
What dread hand? And what dread feet?

What the hammer? What the chain?
In what furnace was thy brain?
What the anvil? What dread grasp,
Dare its deadly terrors clasp?

When the stars threw down their spears
And watered heaven with their tears,
Did he smile his work to see?
Did he who made the Lamb, make thee?

Tyger, Tyger, burning bright
In the forests of the night,
What immortal hand or eye
Dare frame thy fearful symmetry?

— WILLIAM BLAKE

WILLIAM BLAKE'S MYSTERIOUS QUESTION about the Creator of the Tyger and the Lamb applies to the stock market, too.

The stock market is the Tyger. Investors are the Lambs. (And who is the Creator?)

Too many of us don't get it. Too many of us believe what we've been told: "The stock market has been going up at about 10% per year for over 100 years." We have been persuaded that it will continue to do so for a long, long time.

Are those of us who participate in the great creation we call the stock market merely Lambs that feed the Tyger? Without her food, this financial Tyger will cease to be. She needs sacrificial Lambs. And what about us? If we are going to make a profit in the stock market, hunting in the Tyger's jungle, don't we need Lambs, too?

What is the nature of this mystery, this Tyger we call the stock market? How can we hunt in her jungle and not be eaten? How can we recognize danger? How can we recognize opportunity?

These days many disillusioned investors are beginning to sense that their savings have been offered up as a sacrificial Lamb to the stock market Tyger.

This is the problem pondered in this book. Have we innocently become victims? Is the Wall Street jungle a safe place for ordinary investors to hunt? Or are those who venture into this jungle doing so at their peril? If we are the victims, who is the predator?

And if we have inadvertently wandered into a jungle, how can we survive? How can we thrive? What are the rules?

Let's use Blake's inquiring-mind style of questioning to see if we can bolster up the sagging performance of our investments. Let's try to clarify the mystery of the markets. Let's try to see through the jungle.

Let's try to make some money.

Mystery

This chapter introduces you to the more practical parts of this book. It will help you develop a healthy scepticism about the investment industry. It will help you focus on the art of making money and not on the latest, greatest story from some salesman's research department.

Healthy scepticism will increase your long-term rate of return by enabling you to not lose your money. It will protect you from being the Lamb in the stock market forests of the night.

THE MODERN STOCK MARKET is one of the great mysteries of the human mind. What other human creation contains so many ironies, so many contradictions, and so many experts who disagree with one another so enthusiastically? Ironically, the best time ever to have bought the stock market was in the midst of the worst economic depression of the last century. (In 1932 the Dow Jones Industrial Index dipped below 40.) And the best time ever to have sold out was during the longest economic boom of the modern era. (In 2000 it reached over 11,000.) Contrarily, the market rises when the fewest people are invested in stocks and falls when the most people are involved. (In 1932 less than 10% of the public were owners of stocks. In 2000 over 50% of the public were in.)

Interestingly enough, the stock market is most valuable when the authorities disapprove, and least valuable when they most approve. (In 1932, at "the bottom," government officials were outraged at the disgusting way the stock market was structured, vowing to bring forth reform legislation to straighten up the mess. But in 2000, at "the top," expert money managers endorsed the market by investing over 70% of funded pension plans in it.)

HOW DID IT BEGIN?

What kind of human mind could have created such a dichotomy as the modern stock market? No power-crazed socialist politician could ever have concocted a more efficient device for the redistribution of wealth. No genius playwright or novelist could have ever composed more compelling stories than those spun by the stockbrokers of today's securities industry. No preacher, no guru, no philosopher could ever have inspired more hope for the future than is held by today's ill-fated mutual fund investors.

What kind of person could have invented the stock market?

WHO IS THE CREATOR?

Salesmen.

Salesmen invented the stock market for their own benefit. Salesmen operate and maintain the stock market for their own benefit, even now.

Those who study the history of the stock market will discover that it was concocted hundreds of years ago to provide "liquidity" for European speculators in venture capital enterprises. Partnerships, joint ventures, or share companies were created by speculators interested in funding the spice ships, trade route explorations, and the slave business. But once a speculator owned a share of such a venture, he sometimes had difficulty selling his interest and getting his money back. In response to this need, the enterprising salesmen of those eras invented "exchanges," which have evolved into today's high-tech stock market.

Stock exchanges are owned and operated by their members. They're something like clubs. And they are regulated by what lawyers call SROs, or Self-Regulating Organizations. The stock market is owned by salesmen, operated by salesmen, and regulated by salesmen.

SOLVING THE MYSTERY

In order to understand the mysteries of the stock market, we need to understand salesmanship. What makes salesmen tick? That's what makes the stock market tick. Why do salesmen do what they do? That's why the stock market does what it does.

Securities salesmen love making money. The stock market is all about making money. Successful salesmen are intelligent, confident, positive people. They are full of logical, reassuring reasons why stock prices will continue to go up. Salesmen apply pressure to their clients: pressure to buy or pressure to sell. That's what creates the stock market's trading volume and price fluctuations.

In order to make money in the stock market, we must understand the "salesman" aspect of the stock market. And there is one aspect of the salesman's craft in particular that holds the key.

THE ART OF THE SALESMAN

The salesman's art is the art of persuasion. We call it the Art of Bullmanship. This one skill separates the great salesman from the not-so-great salesman. A salesman's ability to persuade clients to follow his advice determines the size of his paycheck. In the money business, it's size that counts. And size is determined by a salesman's mettle in the art of persuasion.

There are two parts to every salesman's job. He is expected to persuade non-clients to become clients (it's called prospecting) and to persuade clients to follow his advice (it's called client service). Salesmen come in a variety of shapes and sizes. One salesman might be called the president of the firm, a director, a manager. Another might be called a researcher, an analyst, a financial advisor, a financial planner, a money manager, an investment advisor, whatever.

Some salesmen are loners; others operate as members of a sophisticated team. But if any of these people's jobs is to persuade investors to become clients and/or persuade clients to follow their advice, they are selling. And understanding the salesman's language of persuasion is crucial to lifting the veil of mystery from the stock market.

Because of the persuasive nature of what all the various salesmen say, all "facts" in the stock market are suspect. These so-called facts are not reported to us for their informational value but are presented to us to persuade us to do something. Stock market research reports or analysts' reports always conclude with a recommendation to do something. They are all persuasive. And they all seem to be factual. But how can a non-expert tell which facts are accurate, which facts are relevant, which facts have been left out, and which facts are simply persuasive bullmanship?

THE 50% GUARANTEE

Sometimes in order to see the essence of something mysterious we need to strip away the complexities and look for something simple. In some cases, we should even oversimplify.

In this case, let's try to examine the factual accuracy of some salesman's stock recommendation. To make it easier, let's oversimplify: Let's look at the theoretical accuracy of all stock recommendations made in the securities industry. Let's use our imaginations to help us untie the knot.

Imagine that there was some objective way to measure the "accuracy of content" in a given securities report: a way to measure what percentage of a given sales pitch is factual and what is merely persuasive bullmanship. Suppose we receive a call from our stockbroker recommending the purchase of ABC Technology Corp. shares, and our broker's pitch is 100% accurate according to our accuracy of content scale. Because of our broker's recommendation, we decide to buy ABC shares.

(We apologize for the ludicrous nature of this exercise. Experienced investors and industry professionals know that no sales pitch or research report is ever 100% accurate. In fact, stock market research reports are always followed by a disclaimer, a tiny-lettered warning to the reader that the brokerage firm is not liable for inaccuracies or omissions. Nevertheless, we'd like to use this fairy tale accuracy scale to illustrate our point. Our point is that the theoretical maximum overall "accuracy of content" for the whole securities industry can never be over 50%.)

OK ... so we're going to buy ABC shares based on our broker's recommendation.

FROM WHOM WILL WE BUY?

From whom will we buy the shares? From someone somewhere who has been persuaded to *sell* ABC Technology stock. Someone somewhere will have read some facts and developed some reasons to sell their shares of ABC. Some type of logical sales pitch will have been presented full of reasons to sell — the opposite of the reasons given to us to buy. The facts we considered reasons to buy would have been glossed over or left out of the factual report used by the seller.

The negative sell facts were given to the seller and the positive buy facts to the buyer.

By the very nature of the securities industry, the sum of all its presentations can never be anywhere close to 100% factual. ABC stock is either a good stock to own or not a good stock to own. How can it be both a "buy" and a "sell"? Yet the securities industry as a whole persuades some investors to buy and others to sell; otherwise there would be no transactions. How can we tell if the presentation we're getting is the accurate one or the not-so-accurate one? Fifty percent is the maximum theoretical accuracy of content for any one recommendation. Our point is that facts presented by the securities industry are suspect because they are basically persuasive. The odds are only 50–50 that the particular report you read will be the accurate one.

(Reality check: In the real stock market, we know that persuasive salesmen are not behind every transaction. This is particularly true for sell transactions. Quite often shareholders independently sell stocks for reasons of their own. Remember that the reason the stock market was invented in the first place was to provide liquidity for large investors who want to sell. That's why most securities research reports are buy recommendations.)

In any case, it is not that important for us to determine the exact percentage of the so-called facts in the stock market that are inaccurate or misleading bullmanship. It is important for us to realize that all of these so-called facts are used to persuade customers to buy or sell. For this reason, all stock market facts are suspect.

HIDDEN TRUTHS

The stock market is about money, not facts. This book is about finding hidden truths in the mysterious realm of the stock market.

It is not about facts and figures, or the fantasies of salesmen. It is about making money.

What are these hidden truths that we're looking for?

Our definition of truth in the stock market is "whatever makes us money."

In a universe of money, the truth must be measured in money.

TRUE LIES

We're not looking for facts; we're looking for truth. We're looking for ways to make money in a world where facts are suspect. If we stick to our new definition of truth, we don't care whether the salesman's pitch is factual or not. Most investors are not in a position to question the securities industry's so-called facts. Our truth must be based on making money, not on analyzing facts and figures. If a salesman's inaccurate facts can make us money, then our truth may, in fact, be a lie.

Let me illustrate. Imagine that a large stockbrokerage firm, Goliath Securities Inc., produces a glowing research report recommending the purchase of ABC Technology shares. Imagine Goliath's army of trained financial salesmen calling thousands of the firm's clients to tell them the persuasive story about why ABC Tech should be bought right now. Does it matter if the facts and figures in the research report are accurate? Does it matter if Goliath's profit projections for the next five years are accurate? Does the content of the research report matter at all? Do we even care whether the report is full of mistakes and false assumptions?

The truth about ABC Tech, using our new definition, is whatever makes us money. And in our example, the truth is that all those fired-up commission-driven salesmen calling all those cash-rich clients will create an increase in demand for ABC's stock. If there is an increase in demand for a stock, and no offsetting increase in supply, the stock's price will rise. In this case, ABC's shares could rise during the time the stock is promoted by Goliath's sales force. Investors who buy early in the promotion period can make money regardless of the factual accuracy of the report.

JUDGMENT

The important part of understanding our new definition of truth is that *we don't care about the accuracy of some salesman's story. We should assume it is inaccurate. We should assume it's a lie because it doesn't matter.* We're not in a position to judge accuracy. Nor are we in the business of making moral judgments about our fellow participants in the stock market. We are here simply to make money.

The salesman, in all his various guises, is the central figure in the stock market. We need him to operate and maintain the intricate moneymaking market matrix. But just because he is important and necessary doesn't mean we should believe everything he says.

Our goal is to take money from the stock market and to prevent the stock market from taking money from us. The secrets to successful investing are not contained in some salesman's story. The secrets are hidden. In order for us to discover them, we must look closely at this mysterious entity we call the stock market.

Let's start with the basics: The stock market is about money. It's about money flowing from one hand to another. It's about commissions and management fees, gains and losses, interest and dividends. It's about something the love of which yesterday's philosophers described as "the root of all evil."

CHAPTER ONE KEY POINTS

- The dominant figure in the stock market is the salesman.
- The salesman's art is persuasive bullmanship.
- The stock market is made up of millions of buyers and sellers constantly exchanging money and stocks among themselves.
- There are many reasons why investors buy or sell a given stock. It's the salesman's job to come up with these reasons.
- Ordinary investors are usually not in a position to judge the accuracy of these reasons to buy or sell.
- Our goal is to make money regardless of the salesmen's stories.

> **Definition: In the stock market, truth is "whatever makes us the money."**

Evil

This chapter introduces you to the more brutal elements of the stock market. It will help you develop a healthy alertness and caution about the investment industry. It will enable you to focus on the art of making money and not losing money.

THE HUMAN MIND IS ONE of the great mysteries of the stock market. What other entity contains so much irony and so many contradictions? Consider, for example, the sinister effect of money on the human mind.

Money twiggles the roots of our basest animal instincts. Money problems can make us angry, greedy, fearful. Money problems can make peaceful people fight, make cautious people reckless, make kind people cruel. Whenever we human animals think about our money, we use the lowest part of our psyche. Our wolf-like sense of territorial dominance makes us aggressive when someone takes what is ours. Our squirrel-like urge to hoard makes us want more and more when we should be satisfied. Our cattle-like urge to herd makes us follow the crowd when we should be thinking independently and using our common sense. Our insatiable hunger drives us to take chances when we should play it safe. We manage our money from the darkest, most primitive parts of our minds.

Because this is true, what kind of creature must our Tyger, the brightly burning stock market, be? Does not the stock market consist of the sum of all its participants? Is it not made up of all of us?

The stock market is about money. If all of us resort to the bestial bits of our brains when money problems rise, what kind of collective creature must the market be? The collective base instincts of all of us comprise the overall creature we call the stock market.

William Blake's question about the Tyger may be closer to the mark than we originally thought. It appears that, in order to understand the mysteries of the stock market, we must first understand the darkest parts of ourselves in the forests of the night.

The market, it seems, consists of the collective animal instincts of the Lambs.

This book is about using our instincts and other tools to extract money from the stock market. It is about living in the Tyger's jungle. It is about eating and not being eaten.

Traders talk about developing a gut feel for successful stock trading. Gut feel refers to our instincts. Because most investors are not attuned to their own instincts, and because most of them typically use their basest instincts for investing, they become sacrificial Lambs: dinner for the Tyger.

It now appears that to develop good instincts for making money in the stock market, we need to understand two aspects of the market: the salesman and ourselves. We must understand the salesman because he created the market and he dominates the market. We must understand ourselves because our own instincts collectively cause the market to do what it does.

THE THEORETICAL "ISM"

So far we have discussed the stock market as if it were some kind of mysterious creature, some tyrannical Tyger created by salesmen and made up of the human animal's basest instincts.

But others might argue that the stock market is simply a

sophisticated exchange mechanism, an efficient high-tech device that enables investors to buy and sell stocks.

Mechanisms are governed by the law of cause and effect. The mysteries of mechanisms are the mysteries of science, mathematics, logic, and reason.

Creatures, on the other hand, are governed by laws of survival. The mysteries of organisms are the mysteries of digestion, growth, elimination, sickness, healing, and reproduction.

In order to understand our Tyger, we need to know which laws govern her: the laws of cause and effect or the laws of the survival of the fittest. Is the stock market a mechanism or an organism?

IT'S A TRICK QUESTION

Who cares? Obviously the stock market is both. It is mechanical and organic.

Our goal is to develop skills that will help us make money. In order to make money, we will have to examine both the mechanical and the organic aspects of the market. But our *goal* is not to study the stock market. We study it as *a means* to make money. So if we make a theoretical mistake, who cares? We are not trying to demonstrate how smart we are or how much market theory we know. We are trying to demonstrate how to use what little knowledge we have to extract money from the stock market.

As you read on, don't be trapped by the theory. It doesn't matter whether you think the market is mechanical or organic, economic or psychological, a bastion of capitalism or a rigged con game. What counts is making money. Whether you agree or disagree with the author's theoretical notions is not important. Can you use the author's theories and methodology to make money? That's what counts.

We will soon reach a point in this book where we start to

become practical. Yes, we will discuss stock market theory. Yes, we will present clear economic models of how the stock market works. (And yes, there will be many salesmen and professors who will disagree with us.) None of this is important. Let our success as a writer and yours as a reader be judged by the change in your financial future. If you can learn to use our unique approach to extract money from the stock market, we both succeed. If not, we both fail.

WHERE DOES THE MONEY COME FROM?

Let's examine one of the mechanical aspects of the stock market in order to discover one of the most important characteristics of our mysterious Tyger.

If we buy ABC Technology shares for $21 per share and sell them six months later for $25, where did the $4-per-share profit come from? It came from the person or institution to whom we sold the stock. It did not come simply from "the market." Our $25 per share was paid by some buyer. It doesn't matter if we sell in six months or in 20 years, our profit will come from the new buyer.

The stock exchange is an intricate mechanical device that efficiently delivers our shares to the buyer and her money to us. But it is other investors who pay us our profits. The reverse is true if we buy at $21 and sell at $15. The $6 we lost was paid to the person from whom we originally bought the stock.

The reasons a buyer buys are the opposite of the reasons the seller sells. Over time, in the illuminating sunshine of hindsight, one set of reasons will be proven correct and the other incorrect. But these reasons don't really matter. What counts is who gets to keep the money.

We use this obtusely obvious observation to illustrate a very important fact about investing: When we make money in the stock market, we take it from someone else. When we lose money, we give it to someone else. It's a personal thing between investors.

Please take it personally!

The stock market is not just an inert mechanical thing. The Tyger really is a living creature. It really is made up of thousands and thousands of people taking money from each other. There really are winners and there really are losers.

"WIN — AT ANY COST!"

This inspiring motto of the Royal Canadian Army Corps of Physical Training Instructors (June 1965) applies directly to the stock market.

It's us against them. Let's be the winners. They can be the losers.

It's combat.

It's financial combat.

Success in the stock market means taking money from other investors. There are winners and losers, just as in any other form of combat. This book is about learning to win at the expense of others.

THE FORTUNES OF WAR

Let's switch from the metaphor of the jungle to the second main metaphor used in this book to describe the stock market: warfare. The study of military combat can help us learn about financial combat. And one of the most important lessons in the study of war is the role of luck.

Whether we consider the soldier who stepped on the land mine or the Japanese worker who lived in Osaka instead of Hiroshima, warriors cannot deny the goddess of Good Fortune.

The same holds true for the stock market.

Everyone who has any history in the investment world knows about fate's fickle finger. There are times when our Midas touch turns everything we do into gold. At other times our best efforts seem only to make things worse.

Not only does Lady Luck play a starring role in our investing, but she does so as well in all the other areas of our life's play.

If we take a few moments to ponder our lives, we will easily observe the role of luck. Just look who you got for parents! How did you meet your first lover? Have you ever been fired? All the great philosophers have written about our destiny, our karma, the role of fate, and the unseen hand of God. These observations about the unexplainable quirks of human fortune are true observations. Investing is only a small part of our lives. Understanding when we're lucky and when we're not is an important part of learning the game of investing.

In financial combat, luck counts.

Let's illustrate this point with another oversimplified story. This one is about two investors and good friends. Charlie Abbott and Bill Zucker had the same great stockbroker and the same desire to make short-term capital gains in low-priced speculative stocks. Their broker, Will Lindsey, was a legend. He had been a professional floor trader on the Toronto Stock Exchange for years, and was still an excellent small cap trader.

After two years of trading, the three of them could not understand why Charlie's account had grown so much more than Bill's. Both investors had bought and sold the same stocks recommended by the same great broker. Why was there a consistent difference in their rate of return? Why had Charlie consistently made more money than Bill?

There turned out to be two reasons for Bill's underperformance. Both reasons could be classified as luck.

First, whenever their broker came up with a buy or sell recommendation, he phoned his clients in alphabetical order. Charlie Abbott was always called well before Bill Zucker, and usually got better prices. Second, Charlie was a banker who was always near a phone. Bill was a schoolteacher, who returned phone calls after class. Charlie consistently got better prices for his trades.

Our basic premise is simple: When we participate in the stock market, we are in a financial war zone. Sometimes we will have good luck, sometimes bad.

THINGS ARE NOT AS THEY APPEAR — YOUR CHAMPAGNE GLASS IS FULL OF BEER

In warfare, one side will usually try to trick the other side. If our enemy does not know what we are really up to, he will be easier to defeat. Surprise is a basic principle of war.

The same is true in the high-pressure arena of the stock market. Things are not what they appear to be. In the financial theater, the stage is curtained with deception. The spotlight is on the performance, but the most important action is occurring behind the scenes.

We're not alluding merely to the problem of salesmen's misleading bullmanship. We know that salesmen in all their various forms use persuasive language and data in their day-to-day hustling for business. Their cumulative work can only be 50% straight no matter what.

The deceit problem in the stock market is much deeper than

mere bullmanship. We will cover this problem in detail in chapter three, explaining, first, how the securities industry creates a shroud over its own reality and, second, how individual investors often fool themselves. However, aside from the industry's intentional deceit and our own inadvertent self-deceit, an element of mechanical deceit is inherent in the securities industry.

Consider, for example, how modern open-ended mutual funds are valued. On any given day, the closing price of each stock in a given mutual fund is multiplied by the number of shares held by that fund. All this is added together with any cash held by the fund, and this total is divided by the number of units outstanding. If we buy units on this day, this is the price we will pay. And if we redeem units on this same day, this is the price we will receive. On the surface, this seems fair to both buyers and sellers.

But things are not always as they appear. If our new buyer purchased her units of the mutual fund late in the year, and if the fund had successfully realized some wonderful capital gains during that year, she could have inadvertently purchased a capital gains tax liability. But it would be the new buyer who would pay the tax on the profits made by the mutual fund during the time the seller owned it. The seller of those same units received the same price, but the seller would not pay the tax.

What seemed like a fair price was not really so fair.

Our second basic premise, therefore, is this: Because the stock market is a type of financial combat, deceit is a natural part of it.

CONNECTIONS AND COMPLICATIONS

"The knee bone's connected to the leg bone, the leg bone's connected to the hip bone, the hip bone's connected to the back bone ..."

That's how it is in the world of finance. Everything is connected to everything else.

But the connection is not necessarily a simple, straightforward one. For example, we might think the price of gold would be connected to the price of gold-mining shares. We might think that if gold's price were to reverse from downwards to upwards, this would eventually cause gold mines to become more profitable, and sooner or later, the price of gold-mining shares would start to go up, too.

But in fact the opposite is true. Historically, the price of gold-mining shares starts to go up *before* the price of gold. Somehow the price of gold-mining shares mysteriously anticipates the price of gold. Gold-mining share prices are a lead indicator of the price of gold. The two are connected, but not in the way we thought.

We may also observe that the price of gold is a lead indicator of inflation. Gold prices rise in anticipation of inflation. But strangely enough, the price of gold also rises in times of deflation. The price is connected to the price of gold-mining shares, inflation, and deflation.

It gets worse. Read on.

Consider, for example, the phenomenon of a bull market. A bull market is an overall long-term up trend in the price of stocks. Early in a bull market, the main cause of rising stock prices might be falling interest rates. Later in the up trend, the main fuel that's firing increasing stock prices could be rising corporate earnings. Still later, the main cause could be the hoards of new investors flocking into the stock market. Not only is one financial event connected to many things, but the connections change as time passes.

The warlike world of finance is complex, not simple.

There are many complex financial causes and many complex financial effects, and over time they change. Education in the feisty world of finance is like education in every other field of human knowledge: The more we know, the more we realize how much we don't know. No individual can ever hope to understand all the specific variables that could affect a specific stock's price trend. It's too complex.

We will delve into these complexities in chapter three. We will use our method of oversimplification to look for profitable patterns among the trees in the Tyger's forest of the night. In that chapter and chapter five, we present two models for understanding the complexities of the stock market. If we're going to use the stock market to make money, we have to learn to see the Tyger hidden in the reeds.

In chapters six to eleven, we will discuss how investors should react to the complex "unknowables" of the stock market business.

"BEAUTY IS IN THE EYE OF THE BEHOLDER"

This sage statement tells us about an important feature of the human mind: We all see things differently. Two people can look at the same thing. One may see beauty, one may not. This is how the human mind works.

Perhaps the human mind is like an organic computer, pro-grammed to perceive beauty. One "eye" might be programmed to see beauty in a desert scene, another in a mountain scene, and still another in an ocean view. One mind's eye might see beauty in a Rembrandt, another's in a Picasso.

The same holds true in the financial world. Every stock market transaction involves a seller and a buyer. Each participant sees that same transaction from a different point of view. One thinks the stock is a "buy," and at the same time the other thinks the same stock is a "sell." That's how the stock market works. It seems that "profitability is in the eye of the beholder."

A buyer might see future profitability in the shares of ABC Tech; the seller might see something quite different.

"HISTORY WILL BEAR ME OUT"

Each day in stock exchanges throughout the world, millions of buyers buy and millions of sellers sell. At the end of the day, all the accounts are settled. The question is: Who are the winners and who are the losers? That question is always answered later, as opposed to sooner.

We might take up former Canadian prime minister John Diefenbaker's famous saying — "History will bear me out" — but this doesn't help today's buyers and sellers very much. Stock market combatants must make their decisions *before* history's judgment is rendered. Our goal is to make money, and money is made by making correct buy and sell decisions *before* the unfolding of history. Easy to say, but not so easy to do.

The trick is to see the truth. And the truth, using our new definition, is whatever makes money. Our eye has to be retrained to see profitability and not be fooled by deception or complexity. We deal with this problem of retraining our "eye" in the remainder of this book.

| CHAPTER TWO KEY POINTS |

- The constant exchange of stocks for money is a type of financial combat. Each participant tries to take money from the others: There are winners and there are losers. Be a winner.
- As in military combat, these are the three important characteristics of the stock market:

  - Luck counts.
  - It is not what is appears to be. Deception is a key feature of the stock market.
  - It is complex, not simple.

- In order to extract profit from the stock market, we must see the truth in it, and everyone sees truth differently.

The truth in the stock market is whatever makes the money.

Deception

This chapter looks more deeply into the deception that is inherent in the stock market.

We're taught as children that lying is wrong. And we usually react emotionally when we discover that we have been lied to. This emotional reaction will hurt our chances of making money in the stock market.

By accepting the now obvious fact that most of what we read and hear regarding the stock market is misleading bumph, we free ourselves from the power of deception. By accepting that the finance industry and even our own human nature are rigged to deceive us, we become harder to deceive. We come to more easily see the truth.

And the truth is whatever makes us money.

IF DECEPTION IS PART of financial combat, we must recognize this fact and take advantage of it. Deception is OK. Our goal is to ignore the smoke and mirrors of salesmen's pitches and get to the truth. It's important that we not moralize about the smoke and that we not be judgmental about the mirrors.

We should just focus on making money.

Our first task is to come to an understanding about the smoke and mirrors we're trying to ignore. Of course, the salesman does not want us to ignore his stories. If no one believed his stories, there would be no stock market. (If there were no private soldiers, there would be no war. We can't all be generals.)

This chapter discusses the smoke and mirrors that make up the giant money redistribution Tyger that we call the stock market. We have to see past the market's deception to consistently make money in the market.

In approaching this material, we will stay focused on our definition of the truth. We are not moralizing about or judging the non-truth aspects of the market. The world we call the stock market is a construct of salesmen's stories, of hopes and dreams and wishful thinking. Mixed in with all this bullmanship is the truth. As we come to understand this deception, we will see more clearly how money is made in the stock market.

LIES

There are three main types of lies. These three can be found in all walks of life, all areas of human endeavor, everywhere. Lies are an essential part of modern human experience. Our purpose is not to be negative or judgmental about lying. It is to study lies so we can see the truth more clearly. Our advice: When a salesman lies to you, don't take it personally. Simply stay alert to the phenomenon.

Type #1: The Outright Lie

This lie is a direct, incorrect statement about some subject. An example might be, "The sky is brown." If the liar is wearing brown-tinted sunglasses, a softened version of the outright lie might be, "The sky looks brown." Or if the liar is color blind, he might say, "The sky looks brown to me." These last two soft lies are technically not actually lies. The sky might actually appear brown to a liar wearing brown-tinted sunglasses. But if the liar is trying to persuade us that the sky is some other color than it actually is, he's telling some form of the outright lie. If he is merely reporting some outright lie that some other liar said, he is still lying. ("Our analyst says that the sky appears brown to him.")

Type #2: The Partial Truth

In this lie the deceit comes from what the liar does *not* say. She is trying to persuade us to do something specific, so she simply leaves out that part of the truth that makes her case look weak. "This car was owned by a little old lady who drove it an average of only 15 miles a week." (What she doesn't tell you is that the little old lady never once changed the oil the entire six years she owned the car.)

Type #3: The Embellishment

In this lie, the liar tells the whole truth about the situation, then adds an outright lie or partial truth to it in order to change the meaning. An example might be: "There is a possibility that this company might be sued for umpteen million dollars, but our analyst feels that this is unlikely for the following reasons ..."

These three lies account for the famous judicial oath, "The truth, the whole truth, and nothing but the truth."

But the stock market is much more sophisticated than many aspects of normal life. As a result, the securities industry's lies are much more sophisticated than normal lies. Consider these Stock Market Lies:

1. The stock market index itself is a lie. Indices like the Dow Jones Industrial Index, the Financial Times 100, the Toronto Stock Exchange 300, and the Standard & Poor's 500 are all held out as statistical representations of the overall stock market. But in fact they are skewed toward an up trend. They have a bullish bias.

   The bias comes in whenever the authorities update the index. What they normally do is remove companies whose stocks are in down trends and replace them with stocks in up trends. Over the years, the index may appear to be going up. But if we check the actual stocks in the index, we will see that they are not the same stocks that were in the index years ago.

   This subtle statistical "adjustment" makes the stock market seem a safer investment than it actually is. (It also helps explain why the majority of mutual funds underperform these averages over long periods.)

We call this lie "the bullish bias lie."

2. "Professionally managed stock portfolios help investors make money." This is a commonly touted assumption in the securities industry. The fact is that most professionally managed stock portfolios consistently underperform stock market averages. (The two most obvious reasons are (a) their fees come off the top, and (b) the indices outperform the markets they represent because of the "bullish bias lie.") Many professionals in the industry advertise their expertise and ability to make money for us. But often their success was mostly luck.

We call this "the advertising lie."

3. "Whose-side-are-you-on-anyway?" Goliath Securities recently published a research report recommending the purchase of ABC Corp's shares. Here are several reasons why Goliath Securities may have issued such a report:

(a) Their excellent securities analyst may actually believe that ABC stock will rise in price over the next while, or

(b) Their excellent institutional research department may have received an indication that their client, Big Pension Fund Managers Inc., would like to sell their four million shares of ABC, and the order (and the commission) will go the broker- age firm who helps them most, or

(c) Their excellent corporate finance department may be nego- tiating with ABC to underwrite an issue of umpteen million dollars of ABC convertible debentures, and it would be great to sell the debentures in a rising market.

Research reports are sometimes written to create demand for the stock. But sometimes the author of the report wants to create demand because his firm has a large supply of the stock to sell and does not want that selling to depress the price of the stock. We call this "the conflict of interest lie."

Bullish bias, advertising, and conflicts of interest have been part of the brokerage industry as long as there has been a brokerage industry. They are tools used by the industry to take money from different types of investors. In a financial conflict, it's important to know who's taking the money from whom. In order to protect our money, we have to understand the matrix of false assumptions that the industry presents.

DOIN' WHAT COMES NATURALLY

The basic programming of the human brain will also deceive us in the stock market. In order to see the truth (using our new definition) about the stock market, most investors will have to reprogram their brain. Why is this?

Because the human brain seeks pleasure and avoids pain.

Securities salesmen appreciate this. They package their financial wares to look like instruments of pleasure. (Even the word "securities" is a misleading label for what they sell.) No one appreciates the pleasure of a rising stock market more than securities salesmen, in all their various forms. The bullish bias lie is a lie that salesmen tell themselves because their brains are designed to seek the pleasure of a bull market. Who can blame them for that?

Salesmen are not very good with financial pain. Like the rest of us, their brains seek pleasure and avoid pain. Naturally they like to avoid accepting blame for their clients' financial losses. Their struggle to ease their pain can sometimes lead to even more losses for their clients.

Most salesmen resort to the old clichés and trite little sayings about how good the stock market will be over the long term. Their lies usually take the form of bullish bias or advertising: "The market will go back up," or "Our all-star research team recommends holding ... We're in for the long term."

"JUST THE FACTS, MA'AM"

It turns out he never actually said these words, but everyone remembers Sergeant Joe Friday of the 1950s television detective series *Dragnet*. When he questioned an overly excited witness, he sometimes got too much excitement and not enough facts.

Modern investors are in the same position as Sergeant Friday. We may ask all the right questions of the securities industry, but the securities salesmen, in all their various forms, will consistently present us with an overly bullish interpretation of the facts. (Bullish bias lies.) And they will consistently remind us why they are eminently qualified to make such positive optimistic statements. (Advertising lies.)

How can we discover "just the facts, ma'am"?

We can't.

We just have to learn to live with the lies.

| CHAPTER THREE KEY POINTS |

- Because of the persuasive nature of the securities industry, it is, by definition, about deception.

- The three basic types of deception are:
  - the outright lie
  - the partial truth
  - the embellished truth

- The three lies inherent in the securities industry are:
  - bullish bias
  - advertising
  - conflict of interest

- Our very nature as human beings causes us to be deceived when dealing in the stock market. This is caused by our tendency to seek pleasure and avoid pain.

Complexity

This chapter explains why current economic news is irrelevant to us in our quest to survive in the stock market.

*Whenever we hear a stock market story about what the market **will do** because some economic statistic is at such-and-such a level, we know we are being misled. The misleading inference is that the economy can be used to predict the stock market. It's actually the other way around: The stock market should be used to predict the economy.*

*If we ever hear a story of how the economy **will do** such-and-such because the stock market **did** such and such, there is a chance we are hearing a valid idea. Unfortunately, most of this stuff won't help us make money in the stock market.*

This chapter will help us make money by allowing us to see the jungle more clearly.

LET'S TRY TO FIGURE THIS THING OUT

First we'll look at the economic cycle and the stock market cycle to understand how the complex network of industry lies conspires to lower our stock market investment rates of return.

Most average investors have an intuitive feel for the economic cycle. We can feel when things are rosy and prosperous and when things are tough.

Sometimes it's simpler just to leave it at the level of "feeling." But that's not how our modern world works.

Nowadays we believe we should be able to explain everything, to analyze everything. This is the problem. It's the analysis and explanations that contain the salesman's lies and the stock market's deceit.

Sometimes an overconfident investor will assume too much knowledge. He will assume that he understands the complex nature of a complex modern economy better than can realistically be expected. To avoid the unrealistic self-lie of overconfidence, do not delve too deeply into economic theory. Try to *feel* the economy as well as *think* about it.

Our premise is that, in the stock market, it doesn't much matter how we make our money. The only thing that counts is that we actually make money. Let's look at how the nature of the stock market itself prevents us from making money and masks the truth at various stages of the economic cycle.

THE ECONOMIC CYCLE

The intellectual mind measures the economy in terms of its growth. If an economy is growing, it's called expansion, boom times, the up part of the cycle. If an economy is shrinking, it's called a recession, a depression, bust times, the down part of the cycle. But try as we may, our intellectual mind cannot remain objective about it. Economists add subjective emotional overtones to their analysis. Expansion is good and recession is bad.

The expansion phase includes increasing corporate profits and increasing employment. The recession phase features decreasing corporate profits (increasing losses?) and increasing unemployment. Any readers interested in the details of modern economic theory should read any basic textbook for a first-year college or university course on economics. (We strongly warn you against becoming immersed in this theoretical material, however. University textbooks are too heavy and intellectual to be of much use in helping you see the truth of the stock market. Besides, salesmen like to use economic theory as part of their pitches.)

Economies alternate between times of overall expansion and times of overall contraction. Governments like to keep their economy in the expansion phase for as long as possible, doing their best to avoid the recession/depression phase. They have created various government agencies to assist them in keeping the economy under control. There are many university textbooks about how various governments do this, too. Again, we recommend that you touch lightly on the theoretical aspects of this heady topic. Government policy is like wind and water. It changes and shifts continually. Economic truth, like stock market truth, is a changing law. What each investor can verify is that, in general, over long periods of time, economic activity swings from good times to bad times, to good times again. Always has. Assume it always will.

The following diagram will assist us in grasping the changing nature of the economy.

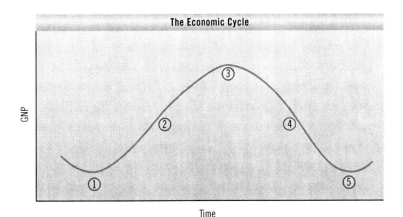

The scale along the bottom of the diagram is "time." Economic expansions and contractions are not as regular in time as the diagram would suggest. A given expansion can go on for years and years, or could end in less than one year. The same is true of economic recessions/depressions.

The vertical scale is overall Gross National Product or Gross Domestic Product. GNP is an average of many, many components. It's only a statistic.

A given expansion or recession/depression does not unfold smoothly the way our over-simplified diagram suggests. As long as an economy has overall positive growth over a 90-day period, it's still in an expansion mode. If it has overall negative growth over a 90-day period, it's in decline.

We have placed numbers along the diagram to give a flavor of what might be going on at the various stages of an expansion or contraction. These occurrences may also change sequence from one cycle to the next. Our purpose here is to impart a sense of what the cycle is like. The economic cycle provides the background for the stock market. If we are to come to grips with the truth of the stock market, we must come to grips with the lies of the stock market. Many of the latter grow out of the economy.

1. Our guided tour of the economic cycle starts at the deepest, darkest depths of a recession (point 1 on the diagram). In these dark days, unemployment will be rising and corporate profits will be falling. Governments will be criticized for allowing the economy to sink to these deplorable levels. The various agencies of the government will be desperately trying to stimulate the economy to get it expanding again. Some of the ways they do this are to lower interest rates or encourage banks to lend money. Government spending levels will be rising in an attempt to fire up the economy's furnaces.

   The mood of the economic community will be pessimistic. The financial press will be full of doom and gloom articles about business failures.

   This is the economy's darkest hour.

2. Months or years later, the economy will be expanding (point 2). Unemployment will have stabilized, and corporate profits will have started to recover. Government agencies will be monitoring the increasingly healthy economy for opportunities to shore up segments that may still be weak, while making sure that the "hot" parts of the economy don't overheat and threaten the longevity

of the overall expansion. The financial press will be reserved but cautiously optimistic. Things will be looking up. Consumers and investors will become more confident.

3. Months or years later, the economy will enter a "peaking" phase (point 3). By this time unemployment will have declined and corporate profits will be healthy again. Government agencies will be trying to cool down areas of the economy that have become overheated. Some of the tools they will use are increasing interest rates and discouraging the banks' propensity to lend money. The financial press will be full of success stories about start-up companies that made it to "the big leagues." The overall mood will be optimistic and confident.

4. Months or years later, the economy will have started to contract (point 4). Some companies will have started to lay off some employees because of deteriorating profits. Governments will be busy denying that there are problems, while their agencies start stimulating the economy. The financial press will report increases in personal and business bankruptcies, offering up many examples of business malaise. The economic community will be less optimistic, and more cautious.

> **Note #1:** When governments try to cool down specific segments of an economy, they try really hard not to send the overall economy into the contraction phase. These agencies are considered to have failed if the economy shrinks. The times when they are successful in cooling down the economy gently without triggering a recession are called "soft landings."

> **Note #2:** The economy falls into contraction when it takes more effort than normal to cool off the offending "too hot"

part of the economy. If the government agencies let the economy heat up too much, it takes way too much effort to cool it off — this is the most common cause of recession. The excess of the up cycle is the cause of the inevitable down cycle.

5. Months or years later, we will find the economy back at point 1.

THE STOCK MARKET CYCLE

The economy provides the background against which the battle of the stock market is fought. It is not our purpose at this time to delve deeply into the theory of why the stock market rises and falls. We will deal with those details in chapter five. Our purpose right now is to understand the source of the myriad lies that make up the stock market. This is an exercise in understanding our own psyche and how we can sometimes work against ourselves in the battle of the stock market. For this reason, we will oversimplify our discussion of the stock market just as we did in discussing the economy above.

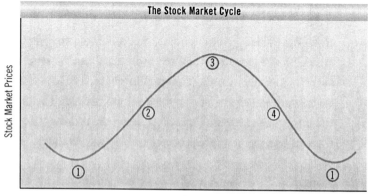

We will divide the stock market cycle into four parts: bottoms, bull markets, tops, and bear markets. Our objective is to buy into the stock market at the bottom and sell out at the top.

1. *The Bottom*

Let's start at the bottom, point 1 on this diagram. The lowest part of the stock market cycle is, by definition, the period when investor demand for stocks is very low and supply is very high. "Supply" of stocks refers to the aggregate amount of stock in various investors' portfolios, where those investors feel they own too much stock. They want to sell off some or all of their holdings. Whenever an investor calls her stockbroker and instructs him to "sell," her stock becomes "supply." Whenever an investor goes online and enters a "sell" order, that stock becomes "supply."

The various reasons for low demand and high supply of stocks at this part of the cycle stem from the very definition of the bottom in the overall cycle: The bottom always occurs after a long period of falling prices. It's no mystery why so few people want to buy and so many want to sell.

This is the period in the cycle of maximum pessimism.

2. *Bull Market*

Two things happen during a bull market (point 2 on the diagram):

(a) The overall level of stock prices rises as demand for stocks increases and supply of stocks decreases.

(b) The overall mood of stock market investors changes from pessimistic to optimistic.

Like the tide, prices rise in waves. Prices will rise, then fall, rise, then fall again.

The rises are generally bigger than the falls and the bull market unfolds in a series of zigzags.

The term "bull market" comes from the attitude of stock buyers when a "customers' man" or "stock broker" calls with a recommendation. During a bull market, buyers would respond positively to the stockbroker's "bullmanship," his sales pitch full of reasons to buy.

During a bear market, the salesman's bullish stories draw grouchy, negative, bear-like responses from the customers. Different mood.

3. *The Top*

The highest overall prices in the stock market occur at the part of the cycle when demand for stocks is highest and supply is lowest (point 3 on our diagram). Investors are pouring money into the market, perhaps even borrowing money to buy stocks.

The top is the time of highest optimism about the future. And why not? All tops, by definition, follow periods of significant increases in the overall price of stocks. Stock market participants have enjoyed great rates of return for a significant period of time. No wonder everyone is optimistic and wants in on the action.

4. *Bear Market*

Three things happen during a bear market (this is point 4 on our diagram):

(a) The overall level of stock prices falls as demand for stocks declines and supply rises.
(b) The overall mood of stock market investors changes from optimistic, to hopeful, to sceptical, to pessimistic.
(c) Prices fall like the tide going out, in waves or zigzags.

There is a certain irony to the stock market cycle. At the bottom, the prevailing mood of stock market investors is pessimistic. This is a period of low demand and high supply for stocks. Yet this is precisely the time when we should be buying stocks. The majority of investors feel like selling, but the correct strategy calls for buying. Similarly, at tops, the mood is optimistic and stocks are in demand. But correct strategy is to sell at tops.

This irony is referred to as the Theory of Contrary Opinion. Long-term success in stock market investing calls for acting in a manner contrary to the opinion and mood of the majority of investors. We have to do the opposite of what "they" do.

But it's even worse than that! Proper strategy also calls for acting in a manner contrary to our own instincts.

We are particularly prone to the herd instinct: our tendency to stick together. Safety in numbers. "The experts can't all be wrong." But the herd instinct is precisely what we must be contrary to if we want to sell at tops and buy at bottoms.

This irony is doubled when we set the stock market cycle against its background, the economic cycle.

THE COUNTERCYCLICAL MODEL

Every first-year economics student learns one important theoretical rule about the stock market: "The stock market is a lead indicator of the economy." This important rule is one of the theories that we suggested glossing over quickly in our study of economic theory. It has little value in seeing the truth about investing. But this rule is very valuable in helping us understand how investment lies work.

The rule states that stock market tops occur before the economy peaks, and stock market bottoms occur before the economy troughs. The next diagram shows how it looks, in theory.

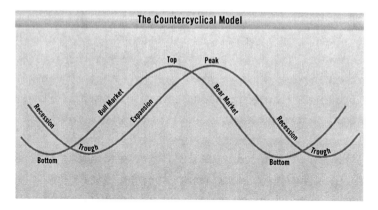

We have lined the two cycles up so that the top in the stock market occurs a few months before the peak of the economic cycle, and the stock market bottoms a few months before the trough of the economic cycle. In other words, the stock market leads the economy, in keeping with first-year economics theory.

Now look at how difficult it is to buy at stock market bottoms.

Stock market bottoms occur as the economy is still deteriorating. Corporate earnings have been declining, and it looks like things are getting worse. The best securities analysts will be predicting lower corporate earnings, and they will be right! At the time when the darkest hour of the economy still lies ahead, the stock market forms a bottom. Imagine the fortitude it must take to buy stocks at this point. To do so, one must not only act contrary to one's own instincts and to conventional wisdom but also to the reality of the economy. It's no wonder that ordinary investors seldom buy the stock market when it bottoms.

Exactly the same thing occurs in reverse when the stock market tops. It tops when the economy is still growing. The best intellects in the industry will be correctly forecasting better earnings and a better economy. The greed part of our emotions will not want us to sell. In fact, we may even be tempted to borrow money and buy more stocks.

"BUT THIS TIME IT'S DIFFERENT"

The most common lie the salesmen tell at stock market tops is that there is some perfectly logical reason why the stock market will go even higher. The industry has always come up with a really compelling story about why either the stock market down cycle or the economic down cycle has been suspended this time. This time it's OK to continue to buy, even though correct strategy in the past has called for selling.

CHAPTER FOUR KEY POINTS

- The Theory of Contrary Opinion arises from the interaction of the economic cycle and the stock market cycle. This theory illustrates why most investors lose money over the long term.
- The theory reflects our human nature: our natural optimism in good times and our natural pessimism in tough times. It is difficult to make money when we have to fight our own emotions.

Objectivity

This chapter begins our explanation of the concrete things we can do to survive in the Tyger's jungle.

Professional traders like to talk about their "edge": about what they have that gives them an advantage over other traders.

What gives us an edge? Objectivity.

Several ancient cultures had methods of teaching the mind how to be objective. In our society, we can associate objectivity with the brain's Reticular Activating System. In a way, it's like a muscle: Use it or lose it.

LET'S LOOK MORE CLOSELY at our notion that the stock market is like a financial war. What kinds of people participate in war? And what can we learn from them?

First and foremost we have the private soldier. The characteristics of a good private are that he is loyal to his cause, brave under fire, does his duty, sacrifices himself if necessary.

Then we have the generals. The characteristics of a good general are that he is cunning, decisive, conserves his resources, strikes at the right time.

In the world of the stock market, we should behave like generals, not privates. **We are generals, not privates.**

Generals do not start off as generals. Most of them start as officer cadets. From a typical class of cadets, very few graduates ever make it to the rank of general. What separates those who make it to general from those who don't is their ability to think and act objectively. Objectivity does not come naturally to everyone. But thank God, it can be taught and it can be learned.

Ancient Viking warriors and ancient Greek and Roman armies had a way of teaching objective thinking. More recently, Japanese

Samurai warriors have shown themselves to be masters of this same type of instruction. Our task in this chapter is to help us learn to be more objective about our behavior in the financial wars. We need knowledge that separates the generals from the lieutenants, much less the privates.

LIES TO OURSELVES

Our simple goal is to use the complex world of the stock market to make money. Our objective reality, our objective truth, is soley based on profitability. What makes it difficult for a human being to be objective is that the securities industry deceives us and we deceive ourselves.

We lie to ourselves because of the way we are programmed to seek pleasure and avoid pain. Let's examine the human brain and see how these "lies to ourselves" reduce our chances of making money in the stock market.

THE FOUR BRAINS

Anatomically our brain was not always as it is now. When we were an embryo developing in our mother's womb, we developed in stages. At one stage we had the characteristics of a fish. At another stage we were like a reptile. Later we became like a mammal and then finally a human being. Our brain was physically different at each stage. As we evolved from one stage to the next, a new brain grew over our existing brain. Researchers such as P. MacLean have studied the link between anatomy and brain function and tell us that we still have the same brains we had at each of these stages, one inside the other, like the layers of an onion.

It's not up to us to support or deny the work of these researchers. Their research has, however, given us an excellent construct for understanding how we think and behave, and that has ramifications for how we invest. Understanding what I'm calling here "the four brains" will help us avoid lying to ourselves.

THE FIRST BRAIN

Our first brain is the intellectual brain. It deals in words and numbers. It uses logic and reason. Modern education is directed primarily toward our intellectual brain. In modern Western society we value it the most of the four brains. But in financial combat, it is this brain that betrays us most often.

THE SECOND BRAIN

Our second brain is the emotional brain. This brain deals in feelings and emotions. It gets excited. It becomes sentimental. It has mood swings ...

THE THIRD BRAIN

Our third brain is the movement brain. It's in charge of fine motor skills and gross motor skills: all the learned motor skills, including talking, walking, reading, riding a bicycle, etc. (Athletes, for example, often have highly developed movement brains.)

THE FOURTH BRAIN

Our fourth brain is the instinctive brain. It controls all of the body's internal processes. It regulates blood circulation, digestion, our immune system, and our body temperature. Primitive urges like territorial dominance, the urge to collect, and the urge to seek safety or shelter come from this brain. So does herd behavior.

All four of these brains operate simultaneously in all of us, all the time. That's why we seem to change our minds so often. What we're actually doing is engaging a different brain.

We are stimulus-response creatures who seek pleasure and avoid pain. Each of these four brains seeks pleasure or avoids pain in its own domain.

Consider a kid in school who's writing exams. His intellectual brain is desperately trying to remember the course material so he can answer the questions correctly. But his cram session the previous night left him without proper sleep and he skipped breakfast before the exam. His instinctive brain is dealing with the pain of tiredness and hunger. It wants to avoid this pain by having him go home, eat lunch, and take a nap.

It's very hard for the intellectual brain to operate well when the instinctive brain is not happy.

Or consider a boxer. The jabs, the crosses, the hooks, the bobbing and weaving that he employs in a fight are being directed by his movement brain. The desire to win is coming from his instinctive brain. Offsetting his desire to win is his instinctive brain's desire to avoid pain. Between rounds, the corner man tries to get the emotional brain to kick in so the boxer is motivated to press his opponent harder. The instinctive brain is sweating to reduce body temperature. The intellectual brain is mostly shut down: It is far too slow to be of any use in direct combat.

We consider investing to be a type of combat: perhaps a type of financial boxing. Is there a risk that, in the boxing ring of investing, our intellectual brain might shut down? Or that, under certain stressful circumstances, it might lie to us? Or that it might believe a lie at certain times and not at other times? Let's review some everyday investment stock market occurrences that might cause problems for our intellectual capacity.

Let's say we bought a stock for $45 per share and one month later it's trading at $40. Our instinctive brain will have difficulty with this. The twiggle in our stomach that accompanies our realization that we have lost $5 per share is an instinctive reaction. Sometimes the instinctive brain will be "helped" by the emotional brain to develop a feeling of anger or frustration. These negative feelings are not problems in and of themselves. But they are painful. And, as we know, our four brains try to avoid pain. This is what creates the problem of self-deception.

Sometimes our intellectual brain will try to ease the pain of the instinctive and emotional brains by making up a lie. "My stock will come back." What if we decided to call our stockbroker as a way of easing the pain? Our intellectual brain might believe his lies: "Our analyst believes the stock will come back next week when the earnings report is released." Perhaps our intellectual brain will be so anxious to avoid facing this painful, stressful situation that it will become convinced to average down: to buy more shares now that the price is lower so that our average cost per share will be below $45.

In this situation, our intellectual brain is trying to avoid the pain caused by:

(a) our instinctive need to preserve what's ours, and
(b) our emotional frustration with things that go wrong.

But let's face it: We are lying to ourselves. Our intellectual brain is telling us lies — and believing the lies — in order to ease the pain. Inevitably, this phenomenon eventually results in more pain, as our stock continues its decline and our long-term rates of return continue to suffer.

The biggest victims of the pain-reducing lie are industry professionals: investment managers and salesmen. They are accountable to their customers for making profit in the stock market and suffer the most emotional pain when things go wrong. If an investment manager or broker puts ABC Corp's shares into 50 portfolios, she may have 50 calls from 50 angry investors when the stock drops from $45 to $40.

Imagine what pain those 50 calls must bring to her emotional brain.

Imagine how desperate she must be for a great intellectual story to relieve her pain and the pain of her clients. Her motivation to lie might be double or triple that of an ordinary investor.

Perhaps this broker can contrive not only to avert her own pain but also to reverse her clients' pain, and so effectively that she actually feels pleasure. It is quite pleasurable to be able to calm someone down and make them feel good. Every mother knows how a gentle, reassuring lie can help her children through some of those tough emotional times that all children experience. "There, there, you'll be all right. I'll kiss it and make it better." This is the power of a great story in the stock market. This is the power of a great lie: It makes everyone feel good.

It's important for us to pause and observe our four brains in action. Try to objectively see them interacting. Notice what your intellectual brain thinks about when your instinctive part is hungry. Notice what happens to your emotions when you are sexually aroused. Notice, when you are emotionally depressed, how difficult is to stand tall, shoulders back, chin up — and how strange it feels, when you are cheerful, to sit leaning forward, head hung low. The four brains are independent, but interconnected. Each has its own agenda, yet each affects the other three.

Success in battle requires accurate and objective perceptions of what is truly going on and of the appropriate reactions. Lies from within our own natural psyche can prevent us from doing this. The interaction of the four brain functions is inherent to all of us. This interaction is an important source of deceit in our battle for financial success.

THE FIFTH BRAIN

We have observed that the human brain actually consists of several brains, one inside the other, like the layers of an onion. One brain controls our base instincts, body functions, and senses, one our learned motor skills, one our emotions, and one our intellect. Not one of these four brains can ever be objective. All are designed to serve our own well-being. All are designed to seek pleasure and avoid pain.

Many people, from psychologists and psychiatrists to grade-school teachers and parents, have verified, time and time again, the predictable, mechanical nature of these four aspects of the human psyche.

There is a part of human consciousness whose job is to over-see these four wanderers: the Reticular Activating System (RAS).

According to Lindsey and Bone in their book *Neurology and Neurosurgery Illustrated*, "A conscious state depends on intact cerebral hemispheres interacting with the ascending reticular activating system in the brain stem, midbrain, hypothalamus, and thalamus."

Taber's Cyclopedic Medical Dictionary defines the RAS as "the alerting system of the brain, consisting of the reticular formation, subthalamus, hypothalamus and medial thalamus. It extends from the central core of the brain stem to all parts of the cerebral cortex.

This system is essential in initiating and maintaining wakefulness and introspection and in directing attention."

Our view is that the difference between the officer cadets who become generals and the ones who become lesser officers is their "fifth brain," their RAS. A well-developed RAS results in objective thinking that breaks free from the subjective chains of the four mechanical brains. A less-developed RAS results in what most of us call normal thinking.

In order to learn to be objective, our first task is to isolate the RAS from our other areas of consciousness. We need to experience what our own RAS feels like. We'll do this by performing The Watch Exercise. Please stop and perform this exercise now, before reading any further.

THE WATCH EXERCISE

Step 1. On a page of note paper, write the four words "Intellectual, Emotional, Movement, Instinctive." Write the words so that you will be able to make a few notes under these four categories if you wish. Then put the paper aside: You will not need it until step 7.

Step 2. Find a watch with a second hand or an LED crystal that shows seconds.

Step 3. Find a quiet location where you can sit comfortably and undisturbed while looking at the watch.

Step 4. Read step 4 a few times: It is the instruction for step 5.

Sit quietly, looking at the watch for one full minute. During this minute, the goal is to have no thoughts.

This is difficult because your intellectual brain mechanically produces thoughts whether you want them or not. If/when a thought occurs during this one minute, passively observe it and let it go away. Continue to hold the mind relaxed, without thoughts, while looking at the second hand. You may also observe certain sounds that might be occurring. Ignore them and maintain a relaxed, thought-free mind. Other physical sensations may occur. Simply make a mental note of them and ignore them, too. Mentally note any emotions that you might feel during the one minute. When the minute is up, read step 6.

Reread step 4 until you feel comfortable with what you will be doing (and not doing) during the one minute of the exercise. Do not read beyond step 5 until you have actually gone through the one-minute exercise.

Step 5. Do it.

Step 6. (One minute later.) Stay quiet and mentally digest the previous minute. Get out your note paper.

Step 7. Did you have thoughts? (Intellectual function.) Did you feel any emotion? (Emotional function.) Did your body move or fidget? (Movement function.) Did you feel any sensations? (Instinctive function.)

Step 8. Again, did you have thoughts? What part of you was observing the thoughts? Pause and digest this question. What part of your consciousness was observing your thoughts?

The part of us that observes our own thoughts during this exercise is the consciousness of our RAS. It simply observes. It is the only part of our psychological makeup that always remains perfectly objective. It's above the other brains' functions. With training, it can be used to coordinate the other brains to think and act objectively, even in the fevered pitch of financial warfare. This part of us, the RAS, will be our main tool in successful investing.

The RAS has its own sense. Because the RAS objectively observes the other brain functions, its sense is common to all four. The Greek philosopher Aristotle was onto this truth when he wrote about "common sense" as the sense common to the other four brain functions.

We will learn to use common sense to objectively observe both the Tyger (the stock market in action) and the Lamb (our own four brain functions in action).

CHAPTER FIVE KEY POINTS

- In order to invest successfully, we must first learn to think objectively about the stock market. This is difficult because of the way the human brain operates.

- Humans actually have four brains. The intellectual brain uses words and numbers to perform logic and reason. The emotional brain deals in feelings and moods. The movement brain is the center for all learned motor skills. The instinctive brain houses primitive urges and controls body functions. Each of these brains operates separately and influences our overall behavior according to its separate agenda. These are the four functions that prevent us from thinking objectively about the stock market.

- The only objective part of our consciousness (with respect to the stock market) is the RAS. It simply observes. In order for us to learn to think objectively, we must develop this part of our consciousness.

A New Path

IF

If you can keep your head when all about you
    Are losing theirs and blaming it on you,
If you can trust yourself when all men doubt you,
    But make allowance for their doubting too;
If you can wait and not be tired by waiting,
    Or being lied about, don't deal in lies,
    Or being hated, don't give way to hating,
And yet don't look too good, nor talk too wise:

If you can dream — and not make dreams your master,
    If you can think — and not make thoughts your aim;
    If you can meet with Triumph and Disaster
    And treat those two impostors just the same;
    If you can bear to hear the truth you've spoken
    Twisted by knaves to make a trap for fools,
Or watch the things you've given your life to, broken,
And stoop to build 'em up again with worn-out tools,

If you can make one heap of all your winnings,
    And risk it on one turn of pitch-and-toss,
    And lose, and start again at your beginnings
    And never breathe a word about your loss;
If you can force your heart and nerve and sinew
    To serve your turn long after they are gone,
    And so hold on when there is nothing in you
Except the Will, which says to them, "Hold on!"

If you can talk with crowds and keep your virtue,
Or walk with Kings — nor lose the common touch,

    If neither foes nor loving friends can hurt you
    If all men count on you, but none too much;
        If you can fill the unforgiving minute
        With sixty seconds' worth of distance run,
    Yours is the Earth and everything that's in it
And — which is more — You'll be a Man, my son!

— Rudyard Kipling

IN ORDER FOR US TO observe the stock market in an objective way, we need an objective language, a frame of reference that will not trap us in the salesman's world of hopes and dreams. It's easy for a con artist to trick the intellectual brain. It's easy for the emotional brain to get excited about some promise of easy money. And those of us who have ever lain awake at night worrying about our investments have first-hand experience of our instinctive brain's method of operating. We all know what it's like to operate from the subjective mind.

In this chapter, we will develop a language for the stock market that will help our RAS (Reticular Activating System) in its efforts to keep us objective about investing.

THE ESSENCE OF PRICE CHANGE

The first notion about which we must be very strict is the actual cause of price change in the stock market. We alluded to it in chapter two: changes in supply and demand. Here are the four basic reasons why stock prices go up and down. These are our first four objective definitions.

1. If demand for a given stock increases over time without a corresponding increase in supply, price will rise over time.

2. If demand for a given stock declines over time without a corresponding decrease in supply, price will fall over time.

3. If the supply of a given stock to the market rises over time without a corresponding increase in demand, price will fall over time.

4. If the supply of a given stock to the market falls over time without a corresponding fall in demand, price will rise over time.

We apologize for dwelling so long on the obvious, but it's important to be precise about the exact causes of price change. The salesmen will slip past this simple discipline and imply other exciting subjective reasons for stock price changes. For example, "The stock went up because the reported earnings were unexpectedly high."

Using our new model, we know this is not true. We insist that the stock price went up either because of an increase in demand or a decrease in supply. Perhaps the reason for the change in supply and demand was related to the earnings surprise ...

We insist on this nitpicky discipline because we insist on being objective.

The sequence is as follows:

1. Price change is a direct, objective reflection of a change in supply and/or demand.
2. Changes in supply and demand are caused by the subjective reactions of investors.

When investors instruct stockbrokers to "buy" some stock, they represent demand for stock. When online investors click the "buy" button of their stock market programs, and their order is relayed to the stock exchange, they represent demand. This is the objective part of "demand." These investors' various reasons for buying comprise the subjective part.

Similarly, when investors sell stocks, they are objectively adding to "supply." All their various reasons for selling are subjective.

If we can remember this, many things will become clear in the financial world of smoke and mirrors.

"I'VE CHANGED MY MIND"

The *reasons for* changes in supply and demand in the stock market are almost entirely *subjective*. Reasons come in three categories: intellectual reasons, emotional reasons, and instinctive reasons.

Remember that the subjective world is the smoke and mirrors world of the salesman. The subjective world is what we must learn to see right through if we are going to see the truth (using our new definition) about the stock market. Let's start by examining what the salesmen refer to as "fundamental analysis" or "financial analysis." This analysis represents their subjective, persuasive attempt to influence supply or demand through the intellectual brain.

LOGIC, REASON, AND THE STOCK MARKET

Every logical reason for making an investment decision can be reduced to one formula. And we learned this formula in grade school. When our arithmetic teacher taught us long division, he inadvertently taught us 50% of everything we need to know about the stock market.

The Grade-school Formula

$$R = I / P$$

$$\text{Interest Rate} = \frac{\text{Income}}{\text{Price}}$$

Apply basic algebra to get

$$\text{Price} = \frac{\text{Income}}{\text{Interest Rates}}$$

Our "one formula" is a derivative of our arithmetic teacher's definition of "interest rate."

$$\text{INTEREST RATE} = \text{INCOME} \div \text{PRICE} \quad R = I/P$$

For our model we will apply basic algebra to this simple formula. We will use the derivative:

$$\text{PRICE} = \text{INCOME/INTEREST RATE} \quad P = I/R$$

Almost all securities research reports, stories, recommendations, or other salesmen's pitches can be reduced to this simple formula and its smoke/mirror inferences. Here's how it works:

- PRICE (P) refers to the price of a given stock.

- INCOME (I) refers to the income received by the stock's owner (i.e., the dividends) or to theoretical future income.

- RATE (R) refers to the interest rate environment in which the stock is being considered.

   In the previous chapter we referred to the economic cycle as the background to the stock market cycle. In this section we refer specifically to the interest rate component of the economy and its effect on a stock's price.

The I Component

Let's examine the I section of our simple formula.

The basic rationale of any buy recommendation is composed of logical reasons why a stock's price will rise. According to our grade-school formula, if Income rises, Price will rise, too. Income refers to the dividend that an owner might receive. If a buy recommendation was based on an analyst's calculation that company was about to increase the dividends it pays to shareholders, this event would be a logical reason to expect the stock price to rise. (So far, not a lot of smoke and mirrors.)

Where do dividends come from? From the company's earnings. Therefore, a company's announcement of increased corporate earnings might be a logical reason to buy a stock now.

What about future earnings? Is there some indication that, even though a company's earnings may be lackluster now, some future event will perhaps change that? (The smoke and mirrors is starting.) Perhaps the anticipation of that future event might be used as a logical reason to buy the stock now. (Now we're deep into the smoke and mirrors.)

What kind of future event might increase corporate earnings someday that can be used as a reason for recommending the purchase of a stock *now*? That depends on the type of corporation or situation the analyst or salesman is recommending. Here are a few examples:

1. ABC Mines is drilling somewhere northeast of Chibougamou, Quebec. The early results show the possible existence of a copper/silver ore body. If there really is a large vein of high-grade ore on this property, the company's reserves of copper and silver would increase to umpteen million tons. The estimated earnings increase due to this ore body alone is $1.78 per share. The stock is currently trading at 3x this figure and 9x its current earnings. Therefore we recommend its purchase at these levels ... etc. (*Increase in assets of the company.*)

2. ABC Pharmaceuticals has a new drug in the final stage of approval. We estimate that this new product, once it has been released, will capture x% of the market, resulting in umpteen million dollars of increased revenue ... etc. (*New product.*)

3. Goliath Banking Corp. announces its takeover bid for ABC Bank. When the takeover is complete, the new company will lay off 10,000 employees, thereby saving umpteen million dollars per year. The earnings of the combined company will be $x, and we recommend the purchase of the stock now ... etc. (*Corporate reorganization, corporate efficiency.*)

4. A powerful new leader is rising up in the Muslim world. His success is characterized by a dramatic increase in "commercial terrorism," a coordinated effort by extremist factions to undermine the commercial viability of the West. His main tool is spreading software viruses and disabling Internet systems. ABC Virus Protection Inc. has the most advanced virus protection

software in the industry. And XYZ Systems Inc.'s software is the most vulnerable to the current wave of enemy virus. ABC's earnings will be impacted positively by this turn of events; XYZ's, negatively. We recommend that you sell your shares of XYZ and buy ABC ... (*Change in business environment.*)

The **I** part of our formula P = I / R illustrates the component of stock market research that is dedicated to fundamental analysis or financial analysis. It appeals directly to the intellectual brain. This **I** component is used to persuade the investor's intellectual brain that some fundamental change in the company will cause an increase or decrease in share price. The logic of the story comes from our formula, which represents the theoretical effect of Income or future Income on price.

The following diagram illustrates our point:

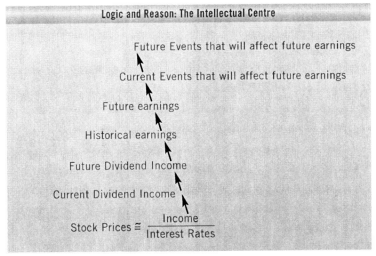

I = current dividend income ➤ future dividend income ➤ historical earnings ➤ future earnings ➤ current events that will affect future earnings ➤ future events. Whenever the intellectual brain is led to believe that some future corporate event will cause a price change, the salesman/analyst is appealing to the **I** part of our simple formula. Increase in **I** means increase in **P** ... and it's the expectation of increased **P** that motivates most buyers to purchase a stock. The expectation of increases or decreases in **P**, the price of a stock, is responsible for the intellectual brain's impact on supply and demand.

Let's test the formula. After all, those who have been exposed to securities firms' research know that the industry spends millions and millions on research relating to the **I** part of our formula. Most firms spend far and away the majority of their research budget on fundamental analysis. How well does it work?

Consider the charts on the next two pages, by John Carder of Boulder, Colorado.

Chart A: During the two years from early 1973 to late 1974, the average corporate earnings of the Standard & Poor's 500 companies rose about 50% and the price of the S&P 500 declined 45% ... Earnings went up, stocks went down: a reverse correlation.

Chart B: But from early 1992 to late 1993, both earnings and price rose: a perfect correlation.

Chart C: Again, through 1936, both earnings and price went up together. In early 1937, stock prices turned down, but earnings kept going up. In late 1937, earnings turned down, too. Price change occurred about six months before earnings changed.

Chart D: The same thing occurred in 1966. Stock prices fell for about 10 months by about 20% while earnings continued to rise. Then, when earnings finally started to go down in the last quarter of 1966, stock prices went right back up! In the space of only two years, there was a positive correlation between price and earnings, a lead/lag correlation, and a negative correlation.

These examples show how tricky life is in the intellectual world. There are correlations between price and earnings, but, as we mentioned in chapter one, the correlation constantly changes. It is complex, not simple.

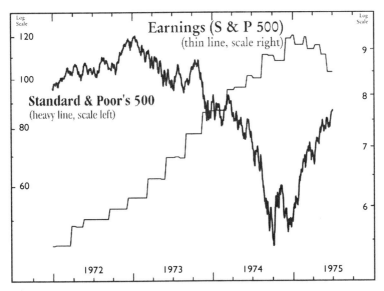

Chart A

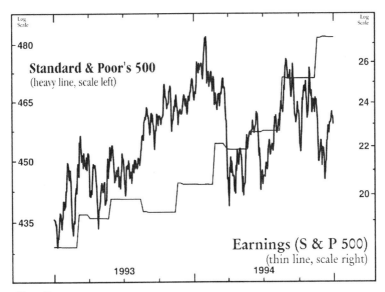

Chart B

Charts copyright © 2008 by Topline Investment Graphics.

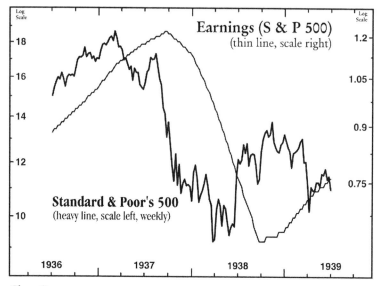

Chart C

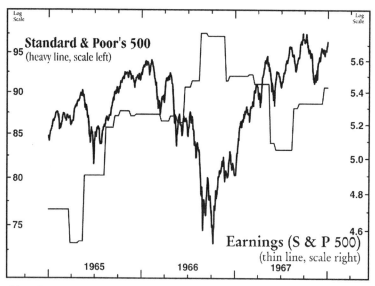

Chart D

Charts copyright © 2008 by Topline Investment Graphics.

The R Component

Let's turn our attention to the **R** part of our simple formula. Logically, if interest Rates increase, Price declines. Conversely, if interest Rates decline, Prices rise. The formula states that stocks decline in price in times of rising interest rates and rise in times of declining interest rates. A 1981 study by Dr. Joseph P. Kairys, Jr., of the University of Western Ontario confirms this notion, using the rigors of academia.* His study shows that there is a correlation between stock markets and commercial paper interest rates.

R is Rate of return or interest Rates available in the overall economy. What causes changes in interest rates? According to various economic theories, inflation would be a good indicator: High inflation produces high interest rates and vice versa. Salesmen/analysts might use their outlook for lower inflation and hence lower interest rates as a reason for an investor to buy stocks.

And what is inflation? Increasing consumer prices are often cited a measure of inflation. Therefore changes in consumer prices might be cited by salesmen/analysts as good reasons for buying or selling stocks.

Are there any other lead indicators of inflation? The price trend of industrial commodities is touted as a lead indicator of inflation and interest rates. Perhaps a securities firm might publish a persuasive report about the price trend of copper, lead, and zinc, and how weakness in base metals prices indicates weakness in inflation, and that means interest rates can't go up just now, and that means it's safe to continue to buy stocks.

Another indicator of the direction of interest rates might be the action of a country's central bank or of the Federal Reserve Board. A brokerage firm research report might state that, because the Fed

---

* "Predicting Sign Changes in the Equity Risk Premium Using Commercial Paper Rates." Joseph P. Kairys, Jr. The University of Western Ontario, December 1991, revised August 1992.

lowered the discount rate twice in a row, this indicates that their intention is to continue to lower interest rates and that it is therefore a good time to buy stocks.

These reports — illustrating this whole set of logic relating to interest rates and inflation and their effect on stock prices — flow from the R part of our formula. We classify the studies relating to the R part as "economic" studies as opposed to "fundamental" or "financial" studies, which address the I part.

Let's check the validity of these economic studies against the realities of the stock market. These charts show interest rates from 1988 to 2008 and the stock market as measured by the Standard and Poor's 500 Index.

Interest Rates and the Stock Market

From mid-1988 until late 1993, interest rates dropped from over 9% to under 6%. During this time, the stock market (S&P 500 index) went UP. Our grade school formula worked.

For the whole of 1994, interest rates went UP and the stock market went DOWN slightly. The formula worked again.

From early 1995 to the end of 1998, interest rates went DOWN again and the stock market went UP again. The formula worked again.

But then the ground shifted. During 1999, interest rates went UP AND the stock market went UP: the opposite of what our formula calls for.

From early 2000 to early 2003, interest rates went DOWN: once again, the exact opposite of what our formula says.

From mid-2003 until mid-2007, it happened again: interest rates went UP AND the stock market went UP.

From 1988 to 1998, there was an inverse relationship between interest rates and the stock market. From 1999 to 2008 there was a direct correlation. If we try to use our intellect exclusively, it is difficult to make money in the stock market. The rules change.

The Stock Market as Measured by Standard and Poor's 500 Index

10-Year Bond Yields / 10-Year Interest Rates: 1988–2008

The P Component

Now let's turn our attention to the **P** portion of our grade-school formula. **P** is for Price. The past price of a given stock can be used as an indicator of future price. The analysts/salesmen who publish these kinds of securities research reports are called technical analysts or chartists. The study of price and trading volume of a given stock over time is called its "momentum." In its truest form, the study of momentum is an attempt to work directly with changes in supply of and demand for a given stock. Technical reports about stock momentum will often use certain terms as follows.

Trend	Price direction over time
Pattern	Specific recurring, recognizable sequences of price and trading volume over time
Resistance	A price at which a rising trend might stop
Support	A price at which a falling trend might stop
Breakout	A price change where the stock rises above resistance
Count	A price "target" of a given forecast

An example of a technical analyst's report might be, "We recommend the purchase of ABC if it breaks out over $30 per share. The stock counts to $37."

A second example of the use of **P** in sales is the notion that stocks will always rise over the long term. The salesman will note that "the average blue-chip American stock has risen an average of 10% annually over the past 100 years. Stocks have always been a great investment over the long term. We expect that to continue ..."

Another type of **P** study is the correlation between the price of a stock and some other price. An example would be the price of gold-mining shares compared with the price of gold itself. These technical studies are categorized as "intermarket studies."

(The author finds it difficult to offer an unbiased criticism of the practice of technical analysis because he holds the designation Chartered Market Technician. There are good technical analysts and poor technical analysts. Our purpose here, however, is not to show that one segment of our simple formula is any more truthful than another segment.)

These three segments, $P = I/R$, represent almost all of the research published by the securities industry: fundamental or financial analysis, economic analysis, and technical analysis. Almost all of the smoke and mirrors associated with the securities salesman's world can be held within this one simple equation. The arguments within this formula are all directed toward the intellectual brain. And the arguments are always logical — sometimes even brilliant. Unfortunately, they are mostly lies designed to persuade you to follow the advice of some salesman.

THE LANGUAGE OF LOGIC: $P = I/R$

Salesmen/analysts use this formula to create the smoke and mirrors of the securities industry. Whenever you hear some story or some salesman recommending the purchase or sale of some security, try to categorize the story using our formula. Most investors do not have the training or experience to judge whether a given securities research pitch is reasonable or silly. Naturally, all the recommendations are made to sound reasonable. Our simple formula will help your intellectual brain remain objective about such recommendations.

No one component of the formula is solely responsible for the balance of supply and demand for a given stock. The fact that a company's earnings are increasing does not necessarily mean its stock will rise. The fact that interest rates are falling does not necessarily mean a given stock will go up. The fact that a stock is currently in an up trend does not necessarily mean it will continue in an up trend.

The intellectual brain is the easiest brain for the salesmen to trick. It subjectively evaluates the logic of a securities story and uses it to evaluate one's holdings of the stock.

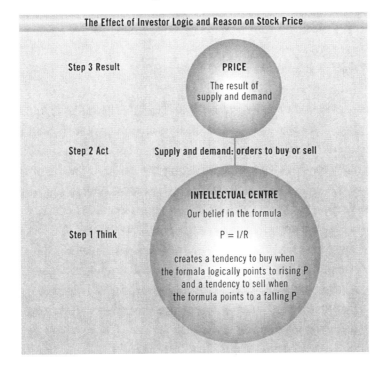

The Effect of Investor Logic and Reason on Stock Price

Step 3 Result — PRICE — The result of supply and demand

Step 2 Act — Supply and demand: orders to buy or sell

Step 1 Think — INTELLECTUAL CENTRE

Our belief in the formula

$P = I/R$

creates a tendency to buy when the formala logically points to rising P and a tendency to sell when the formula points to a falling P

THE TRUTH OF P = I/R AND THE INTELLECTUAL BRAIN

This formula represents the subjective effect of logic on supply and demand in the stock market. The effect of a great research report, a great story, is to change investors' minds about some stock. Their

buy and/or sell orders may then change the balance between supply and demand. And the formula operates through the intellectual brain.

If the stock market was simple enough to be grasped by the
logical mind alone, the $P = I / R$ sequence would contain its entire
explanation. However, to the chagrin of both the salesman and the
customers, "logic" is only one quarter of the subjective causes of
price change in the stock market.

MARKET SENTIMENT AND THE EMOTIONAL BRAIN

Let's review our Countercyclical Model and the Theory of Contrary
Opinion. (See pages 51–53.) At the bottom of a stock market cycle,
the mood of the investing public is most sceptical toward stocks.
Demand for stocks is lowest and supply is highest. At the top of the
cycle, the mood of the investing public is most optimistic toward
stocks. Demand for stocks is greatest, supply is lowest. These notions
form the very definition of what a top or a bottom is.

The mood or emotional base of investors is called "market
sentiment," and its study is the domain of the technical analyst.

When investor mood is negative, the majority of individual participants in the stock market experience a negative attitude toward
stock market investing. If a salesman presents his buy recommendation to a negative person, there is a strong likelihood that the
recommendation will not be followed. On the other hand, if the
salesman is recommending selling, there is a greater likelihood of a
transaction. The emotional brain influences which kind of stories
the intellectual brain will accept.

What causes mood changes in the stock market?

Some say investor optimism is a natural reflection of rising stock
prices. If the stock market has gone up over the past five years,

those who have been in will have great rates of return and a positive attitude by virtue of having been profitably invested. As this fact becomes more and more obvious, more and more people become optimistic and buy in. Investment success, they say, is responsible for the optimistic mood. (Of course, the converse is true regarding a pessimistic mood.)

Others argue that investor mood is a function of the economy. They would say that participants in the economy get more money by virtue of their success in the economy, and when you have more money, you are more likely to be optimistic about investing. (Again, the converse is also true.)

There is a third group: those who argue that mood causes economic change and mood causes stock market change. This is the

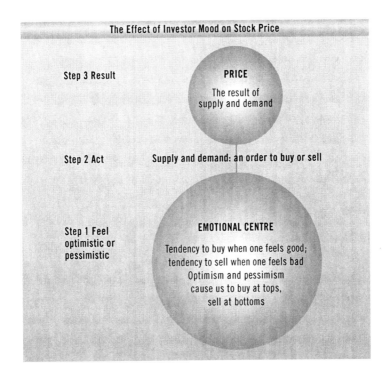

The Effect of Investor Mood on Stock Price

Step 3 Result

PRICE
The result of
supply and demand

Step 2 Act — Supply and demand: an order to buy or sell

Step 1 Feel
optimistic or
pessimistic

EMOTIONAL CENTRE
Tendency to buy when one feels good;
tendency to sell when one feels bad
Optimism and pessimism
cause us to buy at tops,
sell at bottoms

exact opposite of the two previous groups, who believe that mood is caused by the economy and/or the market. Financial astrologers would be an example of this third group.

Regardless of its causes, investor mood is an important part of the causes of supply and demand for stocks in the market. The mood of an investor influences his or her response to the hundreds of intellectual stories that make up the collective sales pitch of the securities industry. Mood comes from our emotional brain.

In contrast to the intellectual brain, the emotional brain is hard for a salesman to trick. How would a salesman make someone feel better about the stock market?

When we want to change the mood of our lover, for example, we might use the right kind of music, a hug, perhaps a caress, a kind word, a sympathetic look. These are not the tools of the typical securities salesman. His training is less effective in dealing with the emotional brain. We are suggesting that a salesman is most effective when customers are already in the mood to buy.

The brain that is safest from the salesman's intellectual smoke and mirrors is the emotional brain. Unfortunately, if we follow the normal mood of our emotional brain, we will buy at market tops and sell at bottoms. It seems that we human beings can create our own emotional smoke and mirrors quite effectively, without the help of the intellectual brain or salesmen and analysts.

INVESTMENT POSITION AND THE INSTINCTIVE BRAIN

In order to understand the subtle, we must first understand the obvious. This was certainly true with regard to the Theory of Contrary Opinion. This core stock market notion uses obvious definitions to come to subtle conclusions. Definitions in answer to the questions "What is a top?" "What is a bottom?" "What is supply?" "What is demand?" lead us to discover that our natural human emotions betray us at the most important times in the stock market cycle. The same is true with regard to thinking objectively about the market. This leads us to look more deeply into the instinctive brain.

The instinctive brain manages body functions like digestion, circulation, the immune system, our senses, and our base urges. In our day-to-day lives, we mostly ignore it. It works quite well without our conscious effort. We do fine without paying attention to the important jobs it does. In fact, there are many instances where interfering with the automatic functions of our instinctive brain will make matters worse. (Have you ever tried chewing your food deliberately? That's when you risk biting your tongue.)

But don't forget about the other important function of your instinctive brain: It houses your base urges. It manages your herd instinct, your territorial instinct, and your urge to hoard or to gather. And if our investing program crosses swords with our instincts in these base areas, we will lose money. Let's look at how the instinctive brain works. Let's see how it affects our investing.

The Herd Instinct

"Majority rules." "Misery loves company." "We can't all be wrong." "School spirit." "My country, right or wrong."

These ideas appeal to a part of the instinctive brain that houses our urge to come together. People with a strong herd instinct tend to be joiners. They'll join clubs, charitable organizations, and political parties. In the investment world, they often prefer to deal only with large investment firms or large banks. For them, size means success. People lacking in a strong herd instinct are thought of as rugged individualists, loners, or even rebels.

The science that addresses human behavior in groups is called sociology. Sociologists study the herd instinct in all its varying expressions. They study the behavior of crowds, the phenomena of riots, leadership, group dynamics, and much more.

In order to understand the stock market, we all need to become amateur sociologists. Remember that the behavior of the stock markets is the collective behavior of all its participants. We must understand how herd instinct is affecting the supply and demand for stocks at any given time. If we see a huge majority of investors all espousing the same wisdom, we have to resist the urge to join the crowd.

The Theory of Contrary Opinion is an objective stock market truth. We must remain objective enough to see through the smoke and mirrors of whatever story accompanies a market top or bottom. The herd instinct will lead us astray if we lose our objectivity.

This instinct often expresses itself as loyalty and obedience. Note that these are qualities of good privates, not good generals.

The Territorial Instinct

Wolves stake out their own hunting areas. Birds will fearlessly defend their nesting sites from other birds. But of all God's creatures, human beings are by far the most territorial. We love our own backyards. We erect fences to mark the borders. We concoct laws to enforce our fences. We human beings have a very strong sense of what's ours.

But we are much more sophisticated than birds or other animals. We extend our grasping sense of "what's mine" far beyond a piece of ground. Our possessions include our chattels, our families, and even our ideas and ideologies! We have laws to protect everything we own. Slogans like "You can't take it with you" pale beside "Thou shalt not steal," and "Thou shalt not covet thy neighbor's (possessions)." "Possession is nine-tenths of the law" may be true, but "possession" is probably ninety-nine one-hundredths of our humanity.

This powerful instinctive urge makes it very difficult for us to be objective about our stocks. It makes it difficult for us to be objective about our losses.

A good general knows when to conserve his strength, when to withdraw, when to back down. Our territorial instinct seriously interferes with our ability to act like generals. Our urge to defend what we think is ours makes us want to fight on and never give up. It makes us act like privates.

The Gathering Instinct

Squirrels collect nuts each autumn. Bull caribou gather cow caribou about them during mating season. Blue jays collect acorns. But again, it is the human being who is above all creatures when it comes to the gathering instinct.

We express our urge to collect as "desire." Our desire to acquire possessions comes from this part of our instinctive brains. A healthy "urge to collect" will result in human being who has ambition and works hard to achieve success. An excessive "urge to collect" will express itself as "greed" and will produce a person whose drive for acquiring possessions detracts from other aspects of his humanity. On the other hand, a person who has a low gathering instinct doesn't care that much about the material things of life.

Unrealistic expectations come from too strong an urge to collect. Unrealistic expectations make it impossible to make objective investment decisions.

(**Note:** Our instinctive urge to collect underlies our desire to make money in the stock market. Our territorial imperative underlies our desire not to lose.)

These three instincts play themselves out when the emotional brain reacts to happenings in the market.

When we lose money in the stock market, our territorial instinct kicks in. It likes to keep what it has. Sometimes we can't sleep at night. Professional traders often advise investors to "sell to the sleep-point." That is, an investor who is uncomfortable with the amount of money she has at risk should reduce the size of her portfolio to the point at which her instinctive brain will let her sleep.

Sometimes we get a sick feeling in our stomach when we lose money. Sometimes we feel a lot of anger or frustration. These are signs that our investment position is out of sorts with our basic instincts. It's very difficult to make objective investment decisions under these circumstances.

When our rate of return is modest and we find out how high other people's rates of return have been, our gathering instinct may engage. It likes to make sure we have enough. We may feel angry or frustrated. Sometimes an investor may feel betrayed by the advisor he has been depending on. Investors in this situation may feel a tremendous urge, courtesy of their herding instinct, to join the stampede of successful stock investors and abandon their less profitable previous ways.

The emotion evoked by our territorial instinct is fear. We're afraid we'll lose more. The emotion evoked by the gathering instinct is greed. We feel anxious to make more. It's hard to be objective about our investing when we're in the grip of these two emotions. But the fact is, most investors do what they do because of these two emotions, greed and fear.

Our goal is to develop a language to help us become objective about investing. Our goal is to strengthen the influence of the objective RAS and weaken the influence of the subjective, instinctive parts of our human psyche.

As mentioned above, the instinctive brain acts out through the emotional brain. Some readers may be confused about greed and fear and the need to follow the crowd. Some might even suggest that these are not instincts but emotions. This is not true. The instinctive brain is quite different from the emotional brain. One difference is that the instinctive brain is very vulnerable to the mumbo-jumbo of a good salesman. Some salesmen prey on investors' instincts. They play on the fear, they play on the greed, and they play on investors' need to feel the comfort of the crowd. Fear, greed, and the need to conform come from the instinctive brain. They are different from the emotional brain's moods of optimism or scepticism.

In order to understand the instinctive brain's influence on our investing, we need to understand just how subjective it is. It cares about what we have. It cares about losses from stocks we own. It cares about our portfolio performance, our rate of return. It will also help us to understand the details of our own investment position. In order to understand the effect of the collective instincts of all investors and how those instincts affect the overall stock market, we need to examine the collective details of all investors' positions.

For example, if we have a lot of cash and very little stock, our fear will be lower than if we have a lot of stock and very little cash. If our stocks are all up, our fear will be lower than if we are losing our shirt. If we have lots of cash and the stock market is declining, our greed will be relatively low. But if the stock market is in a great up trend and we are less than fully invested, our emotion of greed may give us a twiggle. And if all our friends are in the market and we aren't, our herd instinct will cause us to want to join the crowd.

Our instinctive brain reacts to our own particular investment position. It reacts to what we own.

Remember the trader's advice to "sell to the sleep-point"? If a losing position is too big for the instinctive brain, fear will be evoked. By reducing the size of the losing position (i.e., by selling some stock), the investor controls his fear.

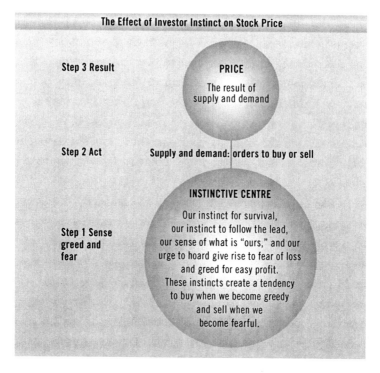

The Effect of Investor Instinct on Stock Price

Step 3 Result

PRICE
The result of supply and demand

Step 2 Act — Supply and demand: orders to buy or sell

Step 1 Sense greed and fear

INSTINCTIVE CENTRE
Our instinct for survival, our instinct to follow the lead, our sense of what is "ours," and our urge to hoard give rise to fear of loss and greed for easy profit. These instincts create a tendency to buy when we become greedy and sell when we become fearful.

Do you see how subjective the instinctive brain is? It only cares about its own well-being. It only cares about its own investment position.

THE HEART OF THE MARKET

Earlier in this chapter we stated that we sometimes have to study the obvious in order to detect the subtle. Readers can easily see the obvious: The various reasons why investors buy and sell stocks are subjective, different for all investors. Our model clearly illustrates this idea. It doesn't matter what we think or feel about the stock market: Thinking and feeling are subjective.

The objective part occurs only when investors actually sell or buy stock. This physical buying and selling is what makes the stock market go up and down. It is the domain of the movement brain. The stock market is a movement-centered thing. Buying and selling — movement — are objective. In order to win the stock market wars, we need to develop our movement brain.

THE FOUR-COMPONENT MODEL FOR THINKING OBJECTIVELY ABOUT THE STOCK MARKET

In the introduction of this book, we used William Blake's poem "The Tyger" to help us see what the stock market really is. And we discovered that it is the sum of all its participants. Now we can look even more closely at this question. Now we see even more clearly exactly what the stock market is. It has four components, three of them subjective and one objective.

The diagram on the next page summarizes the effect of three of our brains on the price of stocks.

The *intellectual component* of the stock market is the sum of all the research reports, all the recommendations, all the financial news, all the opinions, all the sales pitches given every day all over the world.

The *emotional component* is the sum of all the feelings, the doubts, the joys, and the sorrows of all the participants in the stock market every day, all over the world.

The *instinctive component* is the constantly changing effect of everyone's investment positions and our instinctive reactions to these investments.

These three components represent the subjective part of the aggregate we call the stock market. Everyone experiences the ups and downs of the market through these three subjective brains.

The only component of the stock market that is objective is the

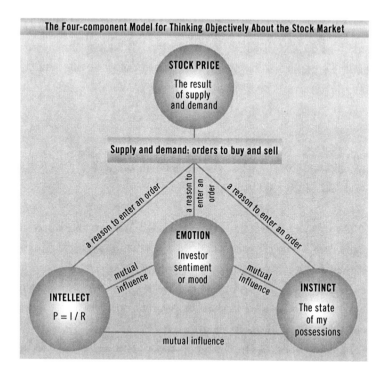

The Four-component Model for Thinking Objectively About the Stock Market

STOCK PRICE

The result
of supply
and demand

Supply and demand: orders to buy and sell

a reason to enter an order

a reason to enter an order

a reason to enter an order

EMOTION

Investor
sentiment
or mood

mutual
influence

mutual
influence

INTELLECT

P = I / R

INSTINCT

The state
of my
possessions

mutual influence

transaction component: the mechanism that executes buy and sell orders. And the minute-to-minute price fluctuations that characterize modern stock markets reflect changes in the flow of buy and sell orders.

The reasons why investors buy and sell are subjective, but the actual buying and selling is objective. The study of reasons to buy and sell is the stuff of privates. The study of buying and selling itself is the stuff of generals.

HOW TO USE THE MODEL

When we visualize the stock market as composed of these four components, we are visualizing the entire market objectively. When we are presented with a sales pitch designed to persuade us to take certain actions, we can evaluate the idea using this model. Deception occurs when we forget about one or more of the components. When we come up with our investment ideas, the four-component model can be used to draw out what we forgot about. It helps us find "the truth, the whole truth, and nothing but the truth."

The most common error investors and investment managers make is assuming that the market is a logical thing. A logical thing can be mastered by using the intellect alone. Imagine, however, what happens if we use only our intellectual brain to make decisions. We become easy prey for the salesmen. They love the intellectual brain. They will present a million facts and figures, all designed to persuade the logic-obsessed investor to buy or sell something. And other salesmen will present another investor with an opposite set of lies to persuade that investor to take the other side of the trade.

There have been many sincere attempts to be intellectual about the emotional component of the stock market. Technical reports use terms like this:

Investment advisory services bullish/bearish
Put/call ratios
Mutual fund purchases/redemption ratios

These are attempts to quantify investor optimism and pessimism. Their strength lies in how they correlate some statistic to objective price levels over time. The salesman/analyst might say, "In the period from 1966 to 1982, whenever the level of bullish sentiment dropped below x%, the stock market rose an average of y% within a 12-month period. The level of bullishness is currently only x − 1%. We recommend moving to a fully invested position over the next few months in anticipation of above average returns over the next year. Specifically, we suggest the purchase of ..."

There have also been many sincere attempts to be logical and rational about "investor position." Technical reports might use terms like these:

Mutual fund cash assets ratio
Stocks as a total percentage of household assets
Aggregate level of margin debt

These are attempts to measure the investor position of the overall investment community. Their strength lies in the attempt to correlate investor position to objectively measurable price levels in the stock market. A salesman/analyst might say, "In the period from 1966 to 1982, whenever the level of cash of cash reserves in equity mutual funds dropped below x%, the market experienced an average decline of y% within a 12-month period. The current level of cash reserves in our recent survey of mutual fund managers is only x − 1%. We recommend a hedging program designed to protect your portfolio from the potential of a serious stock market decline over the coming year. Specifically, we suggest ..."

The problem with trying to use the intellectual brain exclusively is that it wants to find "the answer." It wants to examine facts and come to one conclusion. It often focuses on one or two elements and forgets the whole picture. It works slowly. The stock market is not conducive to this process. In the stock market, the truth changes. The formulas that work one year are scrap the next year. The correct part of the brain to use in investing is the Reticular Activating System.

The RAS simply observes. It observes the conclusions that our intellectual brain comes to. It observes the conclusions that other participants in the market are coming to. It observes what our mood is and what the mood of others in the marketplace is. It observes our own investment position and the investment positions of others. It allows us to enter occasional buy and sell orders objectively. It observes our portfolio performance. Are we making enough? Are we losing? Perhaps another buy or sell order would be appropriate.

The RAS observes the markets and observes our own subjective reaction to the markets. The RAS observes us as objectively as it would observe any other human being. This is how we exercise our RAS. This is how we come to act like a general.

The first difference between a future general and an ordinary officer cadet is objectivity. The second is style.

In the remainder of our book, we will examine the notion of developing our own style.

| CHAPTER SIX KEY POINTS |

- Price changes in the stock market are caused by changes in supply and demand for those stocks.
- There are three categories of reasons why investors enter orders to buy or sell stocks: intellectual, emotional, and instinctive reasons. The price of a stock moves up or down based on the actual flow of buy and sell orders, regardless of the underlying reasons for these orders.

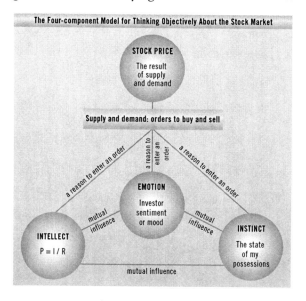

The Four-component Model for Thinking Objectively About the Stock Market

- The intellectual component is represented by the formula P=I/R and represents all financial or fundamental research about the stock market. It is the main tool of the securities salesman.
- The emotional component refers to the mood of investors with respect to the stock market. Investors may be in a mood to buy or a mood to sell.
- The instinctive component is where our instinctive brains

translate their three urges — herding, gathering, and gaining and protecting territory — into the motivating forces of greed and fear.

- These three components represent the three subjective parts of an investor's participation in the stock market.
- The transaction component is the only objective way for an investor to participate in the stock market.
- We use this Four Component Model as a language for discussing and thinking about the stock market. We know that there are three subjective components to any investor's decision to buy or sell.

> Now that we have a model that incorporates all factors that affect the stock market, we are ready for the next step: the development of an objective investment style.

chapter seven

The Five Keys

This chapter introduces ancient wisdom that will help us survive in the Tyger's jungle. Using this wisdom, we will create our plan for survival, the methodology that will help us see past the deception of today's modern financial markets. We will use it to develop our objective investment plans.

We will use it to make money in a difficult world.

We strongly advise you to memorize the five keys introduced here.

THE SECRET TO MAKING more money from stock market investing is to become a better investor. And the secret to becoming a better investor is to become more objective. Our previous chapter outlined certain language that would help us examine the stock market objectively. But objectivity has its price.

That price is pain. As we become more objective, we will experience a certain amount of psychological pain. The truth hurts sometimes. Pain always accompanies the mysterious process by which one becomes humble. That's why so few people ever become objective. The human brain is designed to avoid pain.

ANCIENT WISDOM FOR MODERN SUCCESS

Our method eases the pain by making the process a gradual one. Using it, we will gradually evolve into more objective investors, no longer experiencing sudden, painful shocks.

The particular process by which we will evolve was developed by a legendary Buddhist and Kendo Master of 17th-century Japan.

Miyamoto Musashi wrote his famous *Book of Five Spheres* (also known as *Book of Five Rings*) shortly before his death in 1645. We have updated Musashi's ancient methods and modernized his language to suit today's investors. We will use the terminology of the five keys to investing. For our purpose, Musashi's work is as close to perfect as anything we've ever encountered.

Each of his famous five keys is an area of our own investment lives that we must examine and understand: five separate areas of work. And the work need never stop. The idea is to improve our ability to make money in the stock market by becoming a more objective investor. When we stop the five-key process, we will stop improving as an investor: Our expertise will level out. We will have reached our goal.

If our goal is to become a pro and make millions in the market, then we will continue with the five keys until we achieve that goal. If our goal is to work on our investments for a maximum of one hour per week and earn whatever rate of return we can with that one hour of work, we will stop the process a lot sooner. To each his own.

But if our goal is to earn a great rate of return without any work, the stock market is not for us. The stock market truly is a field of combat. We have to fight to win. If we don't want to fight, we will lose. And if we don't fight, our financial fate will be determined by Lady Luck.

Our methodology makes the investing process more intentional, less dependent on luck. The five-key process is for active, not passive, investors. The stock market is for active, not passive, investors.

Some investors prefer to hire a professional to look after their investing for them. We divide these investors into two camps: active and passive. Active investors want to monitor the performance of the pros they hire. Perhaps they need more than one manager to look after their investments. Perhaps they should fire one manager and replace her with another. This is being active, not passive. Passive investors don't pay attention. The stock market is not for passive investors.

In our explanation of the five key process, we are assuming that you are investing on your own, not through a hired manager. (However, those of you who do use hired help will find it easy to adapt the system for your purposes.)

THE FIVE KEYS

The five keys are:

1. **Know Yourself.** We must each conduct a detailed study of ourselves, our investment history, our financial likes and dislikes, our four brains, the type of investor we are, the type of person we are. Only when we know ourselves will we be able to determine what kind of investing we should be doing.

2. **Your Investment Techniques.** What are our investment techniques? What type of investments do we make? What type of investments do we not make? When do we make investments? What makes us change our minds? How do we close out an investment? When do we close out an investment?

3. **Experience.** "Just do it." Experience truly is the best teacher. As we gain in investment experience, we can revisit the first key, Know Yourself. What do we know about ourselves now that we didn't know when we were less experienced? Perhaps we can revisit the second key, Your Investment Technique, and refine our methods as we gain experience.

4. **Other People's Investment Techniques.** As we progress and learn from our experience, we may examine the techniques of other investors. Should we try something new? Can we improve our own techniques by borrowing ideas from others? Could the activities of other investors eventually harm our position? Should we understand the techniques of others so we can react to their actions? Can we learn from others?

5. **The Unknown.** There are certain things that are unknown to all. There are other things that are unknown to some and known to others. There are certain things that are known to some but unknown to us. We live and invest in a world where we can never hope to know everything, and the stock market is part of this world. But in the stock market, what we don't know can cost us a lot of money. In order to engage in the investment process, we must live comfortably with the idea that we can simply never know all the factors that affect our investments. We must understand our own weakness. We must address the unknown.

These five keys cover everything required to help us become better investors. There is nothing more to it. As we regularly and objectively address these five keys, we will evolve as investors. The number of investment mistakes we make will gradually decline. Our long-term rate of return will gradually increase.

The remainder of this book will be a consideration of the details involved in using the five keys.

The present edition of this book is aimed at investors who are currently unhappy with their investment experience. A future edition may perhaps be aimed at investors who want to turn pro or pros who want to become better pros.

Most of the author's 33 years as an investment professional have been spent with individual clients who have a significant portion of their net worth invested in the stock market. Our examples are drawn from this experience. But the five keys are not limited to the typical investor. The five key method should be used by the novice, the expert, and anyone in between. The Way of the Five Keys contains a universal truth. It works for all of us.

| CHAPTER SEVEN KEY POINT |

* A 350-year-old method affords us the best way to learn how to think and act objectively about the stock market. The method has five keys:

(1) Know Yourself
(2) Your Investment Techniques
(3) Experience
(4) Other Investors' Techniques
(5) The Unknown

chapter eight

First Key: Know Yourself

This chapter asks us to look closely at ourselves. It is an exercise in remaining objective. Self-study is a lifetime study.

*This chapter reviews all of the theory in the first part of this book and asks us to apply that theory to ourselves. In a financial war, the general (that's **you**) has to know all the resources at his disposal (that's **you**, too).*

Only by clearly understanding ourselves can we hope to develop financial techniques that will help us make money in the Tyger's jungle.

MUSASHI AND OTHER BUDDHIST philosophers refer to the first key as The Path. They ask us to study where we were, where we are, and where we want to go on our path. They consider this to be The Path of Life.

The ancient Greek philosopher and mathematician, Pythagoras, challenged us to know ourselves. The later philosopher, Socrates, became famous for this same advice. The Greek words for "know yourself" are "gnothi se auton."

The ancient Nordic rune "Hagala-Dagaz" was a symbolic rendering of the idea of self-observation: observing oneself in order to know oneself.

European mystics and modern-day esoteric schools speak of self-remembering, self-understanding, and self-realization.

Self-study has always been an important part of human philosophy.

It seems natural that we start our journey toward objective thinking with a never-ending study of ourselves.

Who or what are we in the investment world?

Modern psychologists tell us that our behavior stems from our genes and our environment: nature and nurture.

Let's begin by examining our level of experience and sophistication as investors.

We all start life the same: as a naked little baby — 100% "nature." But during our lives, we all have certain experiences — "nurture." Our various experiences have the effect of programming us like a computer. And the result of this programming is what we are now. The task confronting us in the first key is to objectively see our own programs.

To begin this task, let's look at the evolution of a typical investor. The objective here is to recognize ourselves on this scale of investor sophistication.

THE FIVE LEVELS OF INVESTOR EXPERIENCE

Level One, The Saver

When we were six years old, our mother bought us a piggy bank and gave us an allowance. We spent 50 cents and put 50 cents into our piggy bank. By the time we were seven, we had a nice pile of quarters in that piggy bank and we had learned a very valuable skill that would serve us well for the rest of our lives. We became a saver, the first and most important level of investing: learning to live within our means and setting aside a little each week ... and watching it add up.

Pretty soon we opened our first bank account.

The author remembers when his oldest son asked for help reading his first bank pass book. There was the first $56 he had deposited when he opened the account. There was the $100 that grandma and granddad gave him for his birthday. And there was his latest deposit of $10. But what was that entry for 45 cents with the letters "int." beside it?

That's how we learn about interest. Free money! We don't have to work for it, we don't even have to think about it, we just wait for it.

Still later, we bought our first savings certificate or CD.

That's what savers do. They accumulate money and earn interest.

This is the first and most basic level of investor awareness: *the saver.*

Some people go through their whole lives at this level. Savers are the base of a nation's investment pyramid. Governments actually keep track of their citizens' savings habits. We know that Japanese and other Asian countries' people save a high percentage of their income. They live well within their means. North Americans, on the other hand, are poor savers.

Savers don't like risk.

Remember how we said there are five levels of investor awareness? Well, investors at all the other levels risk their capital. The saver is the only one who isn't willing to risk his capital. He always wants to get his money back, plus interest.

So if we don't want to put our money at risk we are, by definition, savers.

For us, the question may be: "How can I become a better saver?"

The question may not be: "Should I stop being a saver and become a risk taker?"

Because the saver does not want to risk his capital and the other four levels of investors are at risk, the saver is in a unique position. She is the only type of investor who can validly use the term "rate of return." The reason is that the saver is the only one who can be sure she'll get her money back. "Rate of return" means we invest $1,000 and sometime later we get our $1,000 back plus interest.

If we walk into a bank and go to the savings certificate counter and buy a Guaranteed Investment Certificate of Deposit, we will see in bold letters on the certificate:

1. Exactly how much money we'll get back (the principal).
2. Exactly when we'll get it back (the maturity date).
3. What our interest will be (the interest rate).

The saver can validly use the term "rate of return."

Let's say we walk into the same bank and this time we go to the mutual fund counter. If we buy a growth mutual fund, we don't know for sure if we'll get our principal back. If we ask what our rate of return will be, the sales clerk will show us a table of rates of return that we would have received if we had purchased our mutual funds three months, six months, one year, two, three, four, five, ten years ago. But in small letters at the bottom of the table will be the words "past returns are not necessarily indicative of future returns." For savers, those small letters are very important.

When savers do move beyond saving, the two most common reasons are:

1. Low interest rates.
2. High taxes.

Another common reason is that a saver may have saved so much money that he doesn't mind taking a little risk, in hopes of getting a greater rate of return.

Level Two, The Buyer of an Investment Product (BIP)

Examples of investment products in the stock market would be stocks, limited partnership units, trust units, convertible debentures, and mutual funds.

Investment products are sold by licensed salesmen. The salesmen have their own agenda for BIPs. What distinguishes a BIP from the next three levels of investors is their belief in the sales pitch, "Buy and hold for the long term." (In other words, "buy.")

Level Three, The Class Investor

The motto of this investor is, "Buy low, sell high." At this level the investor buys *and* sells, which is different from only buying.

The reason we call them class investors relates to the different classes of financial assets. Stocks are one class; fixed income securities, such as bonds or GICs, are another class. Real estate is another class. Money or T-bills are yet another.

The class investor understands that there are long periods when a given class of investments does well, and other periods when the same investments do poorly. The class investor wants to hold whatever class of investments is doing well at that time, and not hold them when they are doing poorly. "Buy low, sell high."

Consider a class investor who believes in holding American blue-chip stocks as the basis of his long-term investment strategy. This investor wants to own these stocks when they are going up, but not when they are going down. Her goal is to increase her long-term rate of return by avoiding the market when it goes down.

The difference between levels two and three is in attitude toward risk. The level three, class, investor is aware that the stock market's trend can change, and when it does, she acts. This level of investor is more sensitive to risk than her less sophisticated level two counterpart. The latter pays no attention to the trend until she feels the pain.

(**Note:** The simple truth is that all investments are good investments at the right times and all investments are not so good at the wrong times. It's good investors who make great rates of return over the long haul, not good investments. We have to take the time to become a good investor.)

Level Four, The Focus Investor

Consider this example: The years 1996 and 1997 were great years to invest in the stock market. A class investor might have chosen to hold a stock mutual fund. That is, he held a broad selection of stocks managed by some qualified mutual fund manager. And in those years he would have made an excellent return.

But a focus investor would be sensitive to which type of stocks was doing best and which type was doing poorly. He might have noticed that the financial-services stocks were in really strong up trends, the consumer stocks were in weaker up trends, and the precious metals stocks were in down trends. Rather than invest in a diversified portfolio of all kinds of stocks, he'd focus on the financial-services stocks and the consumer stocks, and not invest in the precious metals.

The focus investor would understand that the same rules that apply to the asset classes also work for the sub-classes and for individual stocks. The focus investor focuses on the strongest groups of stocks within the stock market. He has learned that diversification is not a very good way to control risk. Selling his risky investments is a better way. The focus investor has learned to focus on individual industries or stocks in favorable trends and sell them when the favorable trend is over.

A quick review before looking at the level five investor:

- The level one investor, the Saver, never risks her capital. It doesn't matter which direction the stock market going, her money is never at risk.
- The level two investor, the BIP, the buyer of an

investment product, makes money when his financial product goes up and loses money when his product goes down.

• Level three and four investors, the class investor and the focus investor, make money when the market goes up and don't lose when the market goes down. They increase long-term returns by avoiding risk.

Level Five, The Two-Dimensional Investor

The level five investor adds one more dimension. This investor makes money when the stock market is going up and makes money when the stock market is going down. The level five investor has a certain fondness for investing and lots of confidence. He has experience in a variety of investment techniques over a number of years. He realizes that many of the participants in the financial markets are strongly influenced by greed, fear, and salesmen. They have no idea what's really going on. For this reason, every so often all financial markets go to extremes. When an economic trend goes to an extreme, sooner or later, normalcy will return. For this level of investor, the return of normalcy to a financial market represents opportunity.

These five levels are a good place for investors to start when working on the first key, self-analysis. We should review the five theoretical levels and review our own experience as investors. Our objective is to categorize ourselves according to our past investment experience. Once we identify our level of investor sophistication, we will find it relatively easy to judge which investment techniques we should consider. Determining our level of sophistication should be an objective decision based on our investing experience.

There are, however, subjective reasons why we might identify with one level over another. And those reasons can be very costly. Consider the following two examples.

Some people need prestige. They feel good about being at the top of their class. These investors often put themselves under pressure to operate at a higher level of investor sophistication than is appropriate, just so they will feel more sophisticated. They do this even though it places inordinate stress on their instinctive brain and their emotional brain.

Other people are overly fearful. They will sometimes operate at a level of investor sophistication lower than is appropriate for their investment experience because they are unrealistically afraid of risk. They imagine the higher levels to be riskier than they really are simply because of their own fears. Their long-term rates of return will suffer because of this irrational fear.

Our own personality often fools us into subjective thinking. In the two examples above, the investors' personalities caused them to operate at an unrealistic level of sophistication and will eventually cause unnecessary financial setbacks.

Our "gnothi se auton" exercise must address the potential problems that our own personalities might cause. Let's examine the personality features most likely to cause problems in the investment world.

PERSONALITY FEATURES

We inherit certain basic human features from our parents. We carry these "programmed" personality features through our whole lives. These features underlie our basic human motivation. They are the reason our goals are what they are. But our stock market goal is simply to make money, nothing more. Any programmed personality trait that interferes with our focus on this goal will detract from our success as investors.

It's not our task to examine the deep psychology behind these personality features. Most investors are mature adults and it's too late for them to change what they are. In order for us to become objective investors, it will be sufficient for us to recognize the features we have. This experience is painful enough! Then we will examine how one or another feature may impair our ability to make money. We must ensure that the investment techniques we develop in the second key take into account our own true personality features.

The Willful

Willfulness is another word for stubborn reactions. The willful person reacts negatively to others. For example, a willful investor may receive a phone call from her stockbroker/advisor/financial planner/salesman advising her to sell a stock that is going down. She may refuse to act because she feels defiant in this situation, not because of any facts relating to the investment situation. She is thinking like a private when she is required to think like a general. Her willfulness feature has interfered with her objectivity.

It's not always easy to see willfulness in ourselves. Our friends are usually better at spotting this feature in us than we are.

The Non-existent

Non-existence looks like a form of shyness. One can become non-existent by retreating, not saying anything, not doing anything — by being passive. Modern psychiatrists might describe non-existence as a coping mechanism that certain people use when they experience stress. But our experience with people in non-existence is that they often become inordinately passive even when they are not under stress. For some people, inordinate passivity is a way of life.

Investors with the feature of non-existence will quietly avoid interaction with others. As a result, they are less likely to be drawn into the salesman's world of smoke and mirrors. Sometimes they find it easier to be objective in their thinking but have difficulty following up with the action required to implement their plans.

The Tramp

People with the tramp feature have few principles. They often don't really care about things that other people care about. And they tend not to care about anything for very long. "Why do today what you can put off till tomorrow?" is a tramp saying. "Why do what someone else will do for you?" is another.

Salesmen love customers with the tramp feature. They can be talked into almost anything. And a little while later, they can be talked out of it! They take the notion of being flexible to an extreme. You can tell when you're in the home or office of a person with a large tramp feature because everything is all over the place.

On the positive side, tramp-featured investors can handle loss better than other investors. It doesn't really matter to them.

The Vain

Vanity makes us self-centered and self-important. It's about *us*. We're great, we don't make mistakes, we have the following good features ... (Ironically, the vain often feel that humility is one of their best features!)

Vanity is one of the most common features among investors. Almost everyone reading this book will have it to some degree. It comes disguised as self-confidence or self-reliance. A good securities salesman knows exactly how to play the vanity feature. His sales pitch will be very sophisticated, almost snobbish, in its appeal. His manner will be very respectful, and his sales close will appeal to the decisive nature of his customer.

In addition to rendering us vulnerable to the sales process, the vanity feature also weakens our assessment of risk. A vain investor will tend to think she knows more than she actually does about any investment situation. She will also tend to blame others for her mistakes. The learning process is more difficult for the vanity-infected person.

The Power Hungry

When the power feature is a big part of our personality, we try to rule or subdue those around us. It may be done bluntly like a corporal chewing out a private, or gently like a mother lovingly teaching her child good manners.

All securities salesmen have power features. Whether they are called stockbrokers, financial planners, investment advisors, analysts, portfolio mangers, or any other title, if their job is to persuade investors to follow their advice, they are exercising their power feature. In our experience, the main determinant of success in the commission/fee part of the securities industry lies in this feature. For the professional investment salesman, the stronger the skill in imposing his will on others, the higher the paycheck. In the securities industry, those who cannot impose their will on clients are considered weak salesmen or leaders.

An investor with a big power feature sometimes tries to impose his will on the market. Combined with willfulness and vanity, the power-featured investor can lose huge amounts of money by steadfastly persisting in an aggressive investment technique (non-technique?) that simply doesn't work. It's hard to be objective about winning and losing money for a person who thinks he's right, and the market will *eventually* do what he wants it to do. It's hard for a person to correct mistakes if he thinks he doesn't makes mistakes.

The Naive

The naive will believe anything. They trust too much. Naïveté and innocence are the opposite of worldliness and craftiness. In a world of salesmen, a world of deceit, naïveté is deadly. When P.T. Barnum said, "There's a sucker born every minute," he was referring to people with this feature.

Unlike many of the other features, people who are naïve usually know they are naïve. (There is a correlation between the distance between our pupils and the level of our naiveté: generally, the more wide-eyed we are, the more naïve we are.)

The Mechanically Good

People infected with the mechanical goodness feature take "consideration for our fellow man" to the extreme. For them, helping out is a compulsion. In fact, with the mechanically good, we don't have to ask for help. They will offer it whether we need it or not. They offer even though it may be really inconvenient for them to do so. They just can't say no.

Salesmen love them.

Mechanical goodness is another trait that is difficult to spot in ourselves. It's best to ask a friend or family member about this one. But here are two symptoms to look for in ourselves:

1. Our life is very busy, hectic, too much to do, not enough time.
2. We often feel resentment toward our friends or family for not being appreciative.

The problem with mechanical goodness in the investment world is that it makes us easy victims of salesmen. A salesman/planner/advisor might be perfectly sincere about helping us invest, but may be incompetent. The mechanically good often find it difficult to take action when the time comes to fire their broker. (Firing one's broker/planner/advisor is a normal part of the securities industry. Loyalty is a trait of privates, not generals.)

"MIRROR MIRROR ON THE WALL, WHO'S THE FAIREST OF THEM ALL?"

In Lewis Carroll's *Snow White*, the dark queen looked into the mirror every day and asked this classic question. It's time for us to do the same.

When the dark queen asked, "Who's the fairest ...", she was exercising her vanity. When we look into our mirror, we will exercise our "gnothi se auton" mindset. We are looking at ourselves not to see how fair we are, but how ugly. We're looking for wrinkles. We're looking for weakness.

Please review the investor features above and then look in the magic mirror. Do it every day, just like the queen in Snow White.

If we expect to invest objectively, we must know our own darker side.

But don't expect your dark side to cooperate. The dark side is very good at hiding itself. We'll need to look through the surface to see the deeper truth.

X-RAY EYES

Don't forget about the four brains.

When we look for our weakness, we will experience a certain amount of psychological pain. Our nature is to seek pleasure and avoid pain. For this reason, it's not natural for us to look in the mirror to see how ugly we are. The four brains will rebel. They are like the dark queen, who only wants to see her own beauty. Let's quickly review the four brains to research any weakness there. Let's make sure that the investment techniques we work on in the next key are not at odds with our basic human nature. Let's look below the surface.

THE FOUR BRAINS AND INVESTING

The Intellectual Brain

This brain operates at three levels.

The most basic level is storing data and recalling it when necessary. People who have talent at this level will quote chapter and verse of some authoritative text and automatically ask all the "correct" questions relating to an investment sales pitch. They seem to know it all.

If we use this brain in investing, we will always be confused but think we're not. We will identify strongly with the $P = I / R$ formula and be easy prey for the salesmen.

The second level at which the intellectual brain operates is teaching (preaching?). It likes to explain its stored data to others. And it likes others to accept its data as truth. It has an opinion and thinks its opinion is important. In the business of investing, a wrong opinion can be very costly.

The third level is asking questions, seeking ideas and information, knocking on a lot of doors. When the intellectual brain wonders about some premise, it is operating at its highest level. When the intellectual brain doubts, compares, looks for patterns, it is operating the most valuable way it can in the investment world.

When it thinks it knows or when it thinks it understands, it is in for a fall.

The correct way to use one's intellectual brain *right now*, as a reader of Musashi's Five Sphere method, is exactly the same. We should be wondering which of the investor personality types we are. We should be asking friends or relatives which they think we are. We should do the same a year from now, and again in another year's time. That's how an objective person looks into her magic mirror. That's how an objective person learns about herself. That's how we learn the truth (using our new definition).

The Emotional Brain

This brain also operates at three levels.

At its basest level, the emotional brain is not really emotional at all. Sometimes the emotional brain will go through the motions of being emotional but will not really feel the emotion. A person operating at this level might hug or kiss someone as a ritual, not as a real expression of affection. They are just going through the motions: motions without emotions.

The second level is at the other extreme: expressing emotion in an exaggerated way. Whatever emotions they feel, they feel them *big*. Carroll's character the Queen of Hearts in *Alice in Wonderland* is a great example of this type.

The third, correct way for an objective investor to use his emotional brain is two-fold:

1. *Expressing only positive emotions.* Negative emotions immediately return one to the realm of the subjective. It is impossible to be objective when feeling this way. (Negative emotions are anger, frustration, boredom, jealousy, envy, fear, greed, etc.) Our

investment rates of return, over the long term, correlate inversely with our expression of negative emotion.

2. *Feeling positive with a sense of balance.* It is incorrect to feel no positive emotions, and it is incorrect to feel exaggerated *big* emotions. The late modern-day Irish philosopher Mervyn Brady felt that the most effective way to develop one's RAS (Reticular Activating System) is by experiencing as many positive emotions as one can, in the spirit of Aristotle's Golden Mean.

The more developed our RAS, the more objective we become, and the better investors we can be. Interesting, isn't it? Feeling good in a refined way helps us think objectively. Feeling bad makes us subjective.

The Instinctive Brain

The instinctive brain is both a blessing and a curse for investors.

This brain is the source of the negative emotions of fear and greed. This is the source of the blessing/curse paradox. Like other emotions, fear and greed can be experienced too much or too little. If experienced too much, the emotion of fear can render investors incapable of evolving toward better things. It can prevent self-improvement. Too little fear can make investors unwary of risk. Too much greed can drive investors to take too much risk. Too little can deter their motivation to evolve. Both too little and too much greed and fear are the curse of investors.

The blessing comes with Aristotle's Golden Mean. If we feel a balanced amount of both fear and greed simultaneously, we will be at the correct balance of caution and aggressiveness that all investors should seek. At this level, fear and greed are not negative emotions. They have been converted into the checks and balances of our investing instincts. They help us remain objective in the treacherous battlefield of the stock market.

When the time comes for us to develop our stock market techniques, we must remember to honor our instinctive brain above the others. If our techniques are not synchronized with our instincts, we are doomed to failure. And if our instincts are not felt in a balanced, moderate way, we will always struggle with Lady Luck.

The Movement Brain

The movement brain gets involved after an investment decision has been made. It is responsible for getting on with the buying or selling. It is at stage center when it comes to developing our actual investment techniques. The idea is to have our movement brain efficiently carry out the techniques that we will develop in the next chapter. The mechanics of executing transactions is an important part of investing, though not normally a controversial part.

Problems usually arise when one of the other brains gets in the way. The most common problem occurs when our emotional brain won't let our mechanical movement brain do its job.

Certain inappropriate negative emotions can prevent us from doing the correct thing. For example, "Darn it! I just lost x% in one week! I think I'll buy more shares at this level so I'll have a lower average cost." This would be a mistake if our technique was to cut our losses short, and let our profitable stocks ride.

Or perhaps some exaggerated positive emotion would prevent the movement brain from carrying out its task. For example, "Wow! I just made x% in one week! I'll sell now to lock in my quick profit!" This would be a mistake if our technique was to let our profitable positions ride, and cut our losses short.

THE REFLECTING POND

We mustn't be afraid to look closely and objectively at ourselves.

Everyone who has ever honestly undertaken the exercise of sincere self-scrutiny has found something they don't like about themselves. We will find something we don't like, too. This is particularly true because of the way we approach self-study. We are purposefully looking for our own weaknesses. Only by knowing them can we develop investment strategies that will work for us.

The stock market has a way of punishing those who can't be honest with themselves.

The process of becoming a better investor starts by looking in the reflecting pond and seeing that we are an ugly duckling. The five-key process is designed to help us become a swan.

For us, becoming a swan means becoming objective. It means we will be able to look at our investments objectively and make objective decisions about them. We will act like generals, not like privates. The number of losses we experience will decline and our long-term rate of return will increase.

THE SALES PROCESS

Modern securities salesmen take their prospective customers through an exercise that looks something like our first key, Know Yourself. They call it the "know your client" rule. Salesmen often ask their customers questions about their financial goals, income, assets, investment experience, etc. At first glance, this appears to be a valid approach to setting up an investment plan. But it's not.

The goal of Miamoto Musashi's Five Sphere Process is to help us become better investors.

The goal of the salesman's know-your-client rule is to sell the customer an investment product and not get sued if the client loses money. The first step of the salesman's process is to find out what category of customer you are.

For example, if we are determined through this process to be a widow and orphan type, the salesman will not sell us speculative securities. The securities industry has this process down to a fine art, with their scores of lawyers and reams of legal precedents. Every investment firm knows what they can and can't get away with. All the big firms have internal watchdogs, who make up what they call the compliance department. Compliance personnel are charged with the job of supervising the sales staff to ensure that they follow all the rules.

Experienced investors who have ever filled in the standard industry new account form know how complex it can be. For every question on that form, there is a set of regulations. A well-trained salesman knows how to ask the questions and how to fill in that form correctly. "Correctly" means so it will get past the compliance department. The compliance department is there to protect the securities firm from being sued. On the surface, it seems to be about us. But it's really about them. The whole process has nothing to do with our becoming a more skilled investor. It has nothing to do with our developing better investment judgment.

THE FIVE-KEY PROCESS

To review, the first key involves serious introspection.

Our overall goal is to increase our long-term rate of return by becoming better investors. Because of the smoke-and-mirrors nature of the stock market, the first key is for us to become totally objective about investing. The hardest thing to be objective about is ourselves. The first key is about being objective about ourselves, about knowing ourselves objectively.

The second key of our five-key process, coming up in the next chapter, involves being objective about everything else. This involves serious "extrospection": taking a serious look at the stock market and selecting our stock market techniques. (If introspection means looking at our personal world, extrospection means looking at the outside world. We look at both worlds objectively.)

CHAPTER EIGHT KEY POINTS

- Our first task in knowing ourselves is to look at ourselves objectively as investors and categorize ourselves according to our level of investor sophistication.

- The first level of investor sophistication is called the saver. Savers do not want to risk their capital. They simply want to get a good rate of return.

- The second level is the buyer of an investment product, the BIP. They simply buy stocks, mutual funds, or other investment products.

- The third level is the class investor. They will buy *and* sell the different classes of investments, as opposed to just buying them.

- The fourth level of investor sophistication is called the focus investor. They focus on industry groups and individual stocks as opposed to overall classes of investments. They also buy and sell their investments, as opposed to only buying.

- The fifth level of investor, the two-way investor, tries to make profit when the stock market goes up *and* down.

- In order to think objectively and to develop objective investment techniques, we must come to grips with our personality features. The goal is not to change our personalities, but to design investment techniques that are compatible with them.

- Willful investors react in a negative way to their various investment experiences. Instead of reacting objectively to the events of the financial world, they automatically react in a negative way.

- The non-existent do not interact with other people. They're shy, but at an extreme level.

- The tramps do not care much about investing. They don't really want to do a lot of work on their investments; they don't really care much about the results; they'd just rather not ...
- The vain over-focus on themselves. Everything is about *me*.
- The power hungry like to control things ... even the stock market. They find it natural to be in charge.
- Naive investors will believe almost anything.
- Mechanically good investors find it very hard to say "no." They aim to please.
- It is also important to understand how our four brains influence our investment behavior.
- Our intellectual brain operates at three levels. It is a great storage library of our facts and figures. It has opinions, which it will sometimes defend enthusiastically. It has the capacity to wonder about things, to recognize patterns, and to seek solutions. This last level is the only one conducive to objective thinking.
- Our emotional brain can feel emotions too much, not enough, or in the "correct" amount. It experiences positive emotions and negative emotions. In order to think objectively, we should feel positive emotions — in a balanced way.
- Our instinctive brain is the source of the emotions of fear and greed. In order to invest objectively, we must feel the "correct" amount of these emotions simultaneously.
- The securities industry's know-your-client exercise is different from the first key. Knowing yourself is about learning to think objectively. "Know your client" is about an investment firm's categorization of its customers in order to know what to sell them.

Second Key: Your Investment Techniques

This chapter will help us ascertain that we have processed chapter eight properly. Once we understand ourselves, we can use this chapter in selecting or devising investment techniques that will actually make money for us in the market.

"TECHNIQUE" IS WHAT separates the winners from the losers.

The way the securities industry presents itself to clients denies the idea of investors even having investment technique. The industry is presented as a never-ending series of financial products and services being offered to a wide variety of clients. Clients don't have techniques; salesmen have techniques. Clients have financial needs. Salesmen have products and services to fill those needs. And salesmen have sales techniques to help them make the sale.

What is an investment, or financial, technique?

A financial technique has two parts: (1) observing the financial world objectively, and (2) reacting to it in some predetermined, objective way.

When we observe the financial world, we are looking for something specific. When we react, we react in a specific, programmed way.

An example of a stock market technique might be an employee share-purchase plan. Each month, employees of ABC Co. are entitled to invest up to x% of their monthly pay in shares of ABC at whatever price it is trading at the end of that month. The company will sell them the stock at a price 20% cheaper than the month-end price. Investor/ employees who use this technique would accumulate shares of ABC at a price 20% below its average price over the time that they used the technique.

The "specific event in the financial world" used in this technique is the passage of one month. The specific reaction to that event would be the purchase of $y of ABC stock at a price 20% below the closing price of the stock that month.

Thousands of employees of hundreds of companies use similar techniques to buy shares of their company's stock. Is this a good technique?

If our goal is to enjoy an upwardly mobile career at ABC Co., and if management aggressively encourages management candidates to participate in the company's share-purchase plan, then this is a good technique. If ABC stock is in a long-term up trend, then this is a good technique. But if ABC stock is in a long-term down trend, this is a poor technique. If ABC Co. is a good candidate for a corporate takeover at a higher price, this is a good technique. If the corporate takeover results in massive layoffs, and you are laid off, the technique worked (the stock went up in price), but you lost your job anyway.

The first feature of this technique is that it is useful to BIPs only, the buyers of investment products, level two of our five-level measurement of investor sophistication. If we are any other level of investor, the technique is not good enough.

The problem with this technique is that it is only half a technique. It does give the investor a 20% advantage over non-employee investors, but it has no elements that aim for a reasonable rate of return. Too much luck, not enough intention.

A proper stock market technique involves both buying and selling. And it involves keeping score. Let's look in detail at what makes a good stock market technique.

HOW GOOD IS YOUR TECHNIQUE?

Intentionality

Exactly what are we trying to do? Our technique must be a deliberate attempt to make money in some specific way. And it must take into account the fact that luck plays an important part in stock market investing. How will we take advantage of good luck and avoid serious loss when we have bad luck?

Intellectually Sound

Are our assumptions accurate? Will our strategy work? Or are we betting on a fairy tale? Remember that we are investing in the realm of the salesman, a land of hopes and dreams, a world of sophisticated lies and persuasive half-truths. We have to check all assumptions against reality. How did this technique work in the past?

Emotionally Doable

Can our emotional brain handle the technique? Or will we feel so good about our winners or so bad about our losers that we won't be able to continue using the technique objectively? Will our techniques produce so much stress in our life that our blood pressure goes off the top of the chart? (This is OK only if your goal is to leave a rich young widow behind.)

Does It Have the Right "Feel?"

Our technique must stay in sync with our instinctive brain. Our instinctive brain, if challenged, will react by producing the emotions of fear or greed. If our stock market technique twiggles these negative emotions, it's doomed from the start.

It's easy to back away from a technique that arouses fear. If we feel too nervous, too fearful, too apprehensive, it is relatively easy to close out our investment and rethink our technique. It's not so easy to back out when our greed instinct is triggered. In fact, greed has the opposite effect. Greed draws us in. Whenever we feel too good, too confident, too cocky about any investment, we should rethink it. If a rethink reveals that we are currently enjoying a load of good luck, then OK, the technique is working. But if we feel our technique is brilliant and we are gifted investment strategists, we should rethink it. We are probably overlooking something important. "Pride goeth before a fall."

MECHANICAL EXCELLENCE

The essence of any stock market technique is in its mechanics. Can we actually do what we want to do? Can we execute our technique?

All stock market techniques involve looking for something in the economic world and reacting to it. Some external happening — traders call this a "signal generator" — gives us the signal to buy or sell. Can we actually find the information our technique calls for? How reliable is our source? Do we have backup? Will we receive the information on time? When we receive the information, can we do what our technique calls for? Can we do it on time?

CUSTOMIZE YOUR TECHNIQUES

Investors who rely too heavily on their sense of logic, or who are seriously vain or naïve, are usually overconfident about their investing. If we objectively recognize some form of overconfidence in our-selves, we should emphasize the fail-safe part of our technique. We plan our failures as skilfully as we plan our successes. What economic event will tell us that we were wrong about this invest-ment? What action should we take to prevent loss — or further loss?

Investors who are willful, non-existent, or tramps will have prob-lems actually following their own techniques. If we recognize one or more of these features in ourselves, we must emphasize the backup part of our technique. We will need the help of a friendly "enforcer" to make sure that, when the time comes for action, we act, regardless of how we feel at that particular time.

Investors who recognize that they have the mechanical goodness feature should not rely on others for the implementation of their techniques. They should lean toward the do-it-yourself approach. Often a third party will talk them out of following their planned technique.

Power-hungry investors have the most difficulty with the whole concept of even having techniques. The situation is made even worse when these folk are also vain. Such investors usually have the wildest rides and lose the most money in the stock market. The basic reason is this: Investment techniques tell investors what to do. Power people tell others what to do. They find it difficult to follow because they want to lead. The power hungry might find it useful to work with other investors who have similar styles and techniques. The group should develop a code of honor about following their techniques. Being lax about following their techniques would be a sign that one is "poorly disciplined," i.e., *weak.*

Note: One major flaw in the stock brokerage firms is that their best commission earners, their top salesmen, usually are both power hungry and vain. These high-powered advisors/consultants/planners have real problems correcting their mistakes. This is why so many of their clients lose so much money.

Investors with a strong herd instinct shouldn't be members of investment clubs. Their stock market techniques should take into account some aspect of the Theory of Contrary Opinion. They must be ever vigilant about what the majority of other investors think. They too often will find themselves thinking the same way.

SAMPLE TECHNIQUES

Level One, Saver Techniques

During the 25-plus years that the author was a securities salesman, this was his single most successful technique.

The technique is to own long-term government bonds when interest rates are declining and short-term government treasury bills when interest rates are rising.

Here's what happens: When interest rates are rising, we purchase treasury bills that mature every 30 days. We're able to reinvest the money at higher and higher interest rates during the period when interest rates rise. But the big money is made when interest rates decline. When interest rates decline and we own long-term bonds, we get profit from two sources: interest and capital gain. First of all, by buying bonds when interest rates reverse from up to down, we lock in the high rates for as long as we hold the bonds. Secondly, when long-term interest rates fall, long-term bonds rise in price, resulting in capital gain.

The key to success in using this simple technique is to switch from T-bills to bonds and vice versa at the correct time. Here's a simple suggestion to help us get started. Follow the yield of long-term treasury bonds. When this rate reverses by 5%, switch. Examples: If interest rates decline from 8% to 6%, at that time 5%

of 6% is 0.3%. If/when long-term interest rates rise by 0.3%, switch from bonds to T-bills. If long-term interest rates rise from 4.2% to 5.1%, 5% of 5.1% is 0.255%. If/when long-term interest rates fall by 0.255%, switch from T-bills to bonds.

A further refinement would be the "can't lose" feature. If we follow this formula, when the time comes to sell the bonds, if we see that the price is lower than we paid for it, we don't sell. We simply continue to hold it as interest rates continue to fluctuate. Eventually, as the buy and sell signals continue, we will get one that results in a capital gain for the bonds. That's the signal we act on.

A further refinement would be to use long-term government strip coupons instead of bonds.

As our experience with this technique grows, we may find a better signal generator, one that is more effective at pinpointing the reversal of interest rates. Maybe there is some investment advisory newsletter somewhere with an excellent track record of calling interest rate reversals. We could use it for half of our capital, and the "5% reversal signal" for the other half.

Level Two, "BIP" Techniques

There are no techniques for BIPs. By definition, they don't use techniques. They rely solely on luck.

Our advice to buyers of investment products is to stop being a BIP and start to think seriously about developing an investment technique. All investment techniques involve both buying and selling.

Level Three, Class Investing Techniques

Our first suggestion for class investors is to read the technique we suggested above for level one savers. It is a model that switches from investment class "cash" to investment class "bonds." Most investors do not realize how profitable government bond techniques can be.

Our second suggestion is a technique that was back-tested by the institutional firm Ned Davis Research. It involves switching between the investment classes of U.S. equities and U.S. cash. When the S&P 500 Index reverses by 8.4% from down to up, we use our cash assets to purchase equities. (Different investors have different preferences regarding how to participate in the overall equities markets. Some prefer Spyders, others prefer Diamonds, others prefer equity mutual funds.) We hold equities until the S&P 500 reverses 7.2% from up to down, then we sell the equities and hold cash, treasury bills, or any pre-selected cash equivalent.

Our third suggestion is to combine the first two techniques. We can assign, say, half of our portfolio to the bond/T-bill model and half to the stock/T-bill model.

Some investors may prefer to engage a specific investment advisor to tell them when to switch from one asset class to the next. They may have heard that a particular advisor or investment letter-writer has a great track record. In this case, we would employ a similar technique, using the specific advisor as the signal generator instead of some mechanical signal generator.

Remember the details. A good technique tells us specifically what we will do when the signal is generated: how to place the order to buy and sell, how much it will cost, how we will get the information, what happens when we are on vacation — all the details.

Level Four, Focus Investing Techniques

A suggestion for a level four investor might be to use the equity-T-bill signal generator above, but instead of buying a broad range of equities, buy only the five stocks in the Dow Jones Industrial

Index with the highest dividend yields. By buying only those stocks with higher dividend yields, we hope to earn dividends as well as capital gains.

Other good techniques for focus investors involve "relative strength." Relative strength refers to a stock or industry's performance over time compared with the stock market in general. For example, if the overall stock market went down 2% in 90 days, and the precious metals stocks went up 1% in the same time, the precious metals stocks would be relatively stronger than the overall market for those three months. This statistic is very useful to focus investors who are trying to decide in what parts of the overall market they want to invest. The idea is to own the stocks that are outperforming the averages.

Another way focus investors use relative strength is in the international markets. Which stock markets are strongest of all the world's markets? The international focus investor might participate in only the top three markets in the world, using relative strength statistics.

Other focus investors might buy only the 10 NYSE stocks that have the highest earnings growth rates and P/E ratios under 20x.

Perhaps a more sophisticated focus investor who loves the stock market might buy any blue chip stock trading above its 60-day moving average that has fallen three standard deviations below its 10-day moving average on the day after the first day when trading volume is triple that of the previous day. A sophisticated investor/trader would use a computer back-testing program to see if such a complex technique would work. She would discover, for example, that 65% of such stocks might have doubled in price during the next six months. She would include a set of rules about selling the 65% at a profit and a different set of rules for selling the 35% of her purchases that declined in price.

Level Five, Two-Way Investing Techniques

Ideas for level five investors include ways to profit when the stock market goes down. One technique might be to sell short any stock the day after it first appears on the "new low" list, and to buy any stock the day after it first appears on the "new high" list. Exact rules for when to close out the position would also have to be incorporated into the technique.

Another technique for profiting from a stock that goes down is the convertible hedge. This involves the purchase of convertible debentures and the subsequent short sale of the stock into which the debenture is convertible. This creates a hedge. Since convertible debentures normally decline less than the corresponding stock, the position becomes profitable as the stock declines. And the investor earns interest on the debenture, too. Investors who use this technique must investigate margin rates, borrowing fees, and their broker's policy regarding short squeezes. (The author's single most profitable transaction ever came from a convertible hedge.)

Reminder #1: Level five is for experienced investors only.

Reminder #2: A good technique includes a lot of detail: exactly what we will do in the various scenarios that unfold in the stock market. The more work we do preparing for combat, the less likely we are to become a casualty.

AT YOUR SERVICE

There are hundreds of investment professionals who have written hundreds of books about their own particular investment techniques. Most of these books and advisory services are for investors who have little discipline and no technique. Much of it is salesman's fluff for disorganized investors. But there are diamonds in the coal scuttle. Of course, they *all* claim to be diamonds ...

Over the years, good investment advisors come and go. How can we tell the good from the bad? It's not about how good or bad *they* are: it's about *how useful they are to us* at any given time. It's about *us*. Who are we in the financial world? What are *our techniques*? The good advisors are those who can help us implement *our* financial techniques.

K.I.S.S.

Keep it simple, stupid, is a good principle to follow. When you are drafting your first techniques, don't get too fancy. Start with something simple. Err on the side of being overly conservative. Our techniques evolve as we evolve.

CHAPTER NINE KEY POINTS

• Investment technique involves the investor objectively
  observing the financial world and objectively reacting to
  it in a predetermined way. Good technique has six
  characteristics:

  — It's intentional. It embodies a clear understanding of
    what the investor expects from the complex world
    of finance, and how he will profit from it.
  — It's intellectually sound. In a world of salesmen and
    deceit, the investor must test all of her assumptions
    against reality.
  — It should be compatible with the investor's instinc-
    tive feeling about risk associated with her
    investment position.
  — It must take into account an investor's ability to
    actually do what the technique calls for.
  — It should be compatible with all of an investor's
    personality traits.
  — It will often have to be customized for investors
    with specific personality limitations.

Third Key: Experience

Experience is the best teacher. Eventually you will put down the books and start to apply what you have learned. This chapter discusses some of the pitfalls to avoid once you engage the Tyger.

BY NOW WE SHOULD have noticed an important feature of Musashi's ancient five-key method: We have spent a lot of time preparing to invest, but have not yet invested. Training and preparation for combat are as important as combat itself.

To this point, it has been relatively easy to remain objective. It's not so easy once the action starts. The third key, experience, is the action.

There are three important elements in understanding this key.

The first is that this is where the money is made and lost. This is where we test our own mettle and the mettle of our technique(s). This is the financial combat that we've been discussing. If we don't get this part right, none of the other parts count. Executing our technique demands our full focus and objective attention. The key of experience is where we win or lose.

The second is to remain emotionally balanced. The trite slogan, "It's only money," has a strong ring of truth to it. The emotion attached to winning and losing in the day-to-day action of the stock market has the effect of "drawing you in." We may start to feel too much emotion or too little. The negative emotions that accompany loss become more and more difficult to live with. They sap away our objectivity. And when we lose our objectivity, it's only a matter of time and luck until we lose our money, too.

The third is to learn from our experience. In order to learn from experience, we have to observe that experience objectively. William Shakespeare's metaphor (and Elvis Presley's adaptation of it) is really useful to those of us who would learn from our experience. "The world's a stage" — we are all actors in the play of life.

In order to learn from experience, we have to play our role *and* sit in the audience at the very same time. We play the part of a successful, objective investor *and* observe ourselves in that role, simultaneously. We cannot write the script for the stock market's play. But we can play our parts very well. And in order to be better players, we need to know what areas of our performance need improvement. We use the methods and studies of the first and second keys to show us where we need to work on ourselves.

Many books have been written about investing in the stock market, but no one writes a book about you. You have to write that book yourself. You have to learn about yourself in the School of Experience, the third key.

AUTOMATIC PILOT

When a pilot flies an aircraft, he uses checklists. For example, when he prepares for takeoff, he may have 10 or 20 items to review. (Check the fuel level, check the radio setting, check the altimeter reading, etc.) When he prepares for landing, he may have 10 or 20 other items to check. These checks constitute important parts of his "technique" in flying the aircraft. When a pilot performs these checks, he is fully alert, fully in charge of the situation. He is not on a coffee break with the aircraft set on automatic pilot.

When we are performing the day-to-day or week-to-week activities of "flying" our investments, we are not on automatic pilot, either. Sometimes, when our investment technique has been working well for a long time, a certain complacency can set in. That's how investing on automatic pilot starts. And that's when the trouble starts.

The Tyger loves to catch her Lambs off guard.

As we monitor our investments from day to day or week to week, we should do so like the pilot using his checklist. We are fully alert, fully in charge of the situation. We are monitoring our emotional brains, too, balancing between the correct amount of greed and the correct amount of fear.

BACK TO SQUARE ONE

Experience changes us. As we gain experience in investing in the stock market, we will learn. Systematic learning makes us better investors. (In other words, the five key system works.) As we become better, we can improve our technique(s). Then we can become better at using our improved technique. It goes in a circle. It almost seems that we could become perfectly good investors if we used only the first three keys. And to a point, this is true. If they are the only ones we use, we will improve our investing.

But our investing is not carried out in isolation. Investing really is combat. In financial combat, the other investor is out to get our money, just as we are out to get hers. We'd better understand what the other combatants are doing, too.

CHAPTER TEN KEY POINTS

- As we experience the day-to-day action of investing, we should keep in mind three elements of success:

  — The first is that experience is the difference between reading a book about investing and actually investing.
  — At this point, real money changes hands. This is where we win or lose.
  — The second is to remain emotionally balanced.
  — The third is to learn from our experience. To do so, we must simultaneously play our role as investor and observe ourselves in that role.

- We should never become complacent about our investing. No financial technique works all the time.
- The first three keys of Musashi's five-key system can be used to improve our investment success up to a point. As we gain experience, that experience changes what we are as investors. When we review the first key to know ourselves, we find it is "ourselves" who have changed with experience. Now we are ready to refine and improve our technique(s).

Fourth Key: Other Investors' Techniques

This chapter is a warning. When devising our investment techniques, we had better be keenly aware of other hunters' techniques, too. We're not the only ones in this jungle. We, too, are being hunted.

WE STUDY THE TECHNIQUES of other investors for two reasons. First, there are many investment professionals who have been earning a living from the stock market for many years. Many good people have become wealthy by skilfully using the stock market. We can learn techniques from these people. And second, there are many con artists who have been earning a living from the stock market for years, too. Many not-so-good people have become wealthy by skilfully using the stock market. We had better learn from them, too.

The simple truth is that there are only a limited number of techniques for investing in the stock market. Very few people invent new methods. Those few who do are normally advanced professionals. There is no need for any investor to be inventive. The need is to be objective, intentional, and systematic.

Some people feel it's cheating if they use someone else's idea. It's like stealing. Others feel, "If her technique is so great, why did she write a book about it? Why wouldn't she just use the idea to make money in the market herself?" Or, "If she's so smart, why ain't she rich?"

These negative thoughts come from our emotional brain, based on our personality types. This type of negative, emotional thinking prevents us from evolving as investors. For example, a vain person will have trouble admitting that there are better investors than he. A power-hungry person will have trouble taking suggestions from others. A person with a big fear feature will have trouble trying anything new.

Our own personality can stop us from becoming better at investing. Our own personality can lower our rate of return.

DON'T LIE, BUT IT'S OK TO STEAL

The stock market is all about taking money from someone else: In a strange way, it's like stealing.

We should steal ideas, too. Here's why:

1. The stock market constantly shifts. What works this year will be out of favor next year. We have to keep up with this constant change in order to prevent loss and maintain our rate of return.
2. Our natural tendency as human beings is to remain the same, to be comfortable, to stop evolving. If finding new ideas becomes a difficult, painful process, our evolution could stop. It's easy to buy or steal someone else's ideas and adapt them for our own purposes.

FOLLOW THE LEADER: THE FINANCIAL HERO

The financial press loves its heroes. And they love a good story. Every once in a while, they will write about some investor, some trader, some money manager who has been making a lot of money lately. These financial hero stories are interesting places to start our research on how "the other guy" invests. Unfortunately, many of the press's heroes are oddball types whose area of specialty is so narrow that it's of little use to a normal investor. But even the oddballs have their value.

We remember the stories in the late 1960s and early 1970s about gold bugs. ("Gold bug" is stock market jargon for an investor who "believes in" gold.) In those days, the price of gold had been pegged at $35 per ounce since the 1930s, and there were very few investors who ever even considered it of any interest. Their attitude was, how can we develop a technique to invest in something that never changes price?

But things changed. By 1980, gold became one of the world's most popular investments. During the 1970s the U.S. stock market had gone through a series of huge up and down swings, resulting in poor rates of return for most investors in blue-chip U.S. growth stocks. But at the same time, the price of gold rose by over 20 times.

Shortly after gold had tripled in price from its pegged $35 per ounce to $100 per ounce, the financial press wrote plenty of good stories about their new heroes, the gold bugs. There was plenty of time for alert investors to develop gold-oriented investment techniques based on the techniques of the gold bugs. And of course there was plenty of money to be made, too.

FOLLOW YOURSELF

Most of the techniques we read about in the financial press are laced with the three basic lies of the securities industry: bullish bias, advertising, and conflict of interest. Most of them are offered by a salesman with a great story. Most of what we refer to as "the other guy's techniques" are merely sales pitches for some financial product or service. Most of this is hot air. It's hard to find those diamonds in the coal scuttle.

But there is an important reason why we should study these pitches.

Sales pitches are crucial for our evolution. Musashi observed that we can never really understand ourselves unless we understand others. We can never really master our own techniques unless we grasp what others are trying to do. Or, in our language, we can never really understand how to take money from others unless we grasp how others are trying to take money from us.

At the philosophical level, they say that the reason God invented hell is so that the human mind could understand heaven. The human mind thinks about one thing by comparing it with another. We develop ourselves by comparing ourselves to others.

BACK TO BASICS

Let's review some of the basic ways money is made in the stock market. Our purpose is to ensure that we formally recognize the realities of the financial world and take those realities into account in developing our own techniques.

1. Income investing. The investor purchases a security that pays interest or dividends directly to the investor. The reason for buying is to receive the income.
2. Growth of income. If an investor owns shares of a common stock where the underlying company's business is expanding, the company may have a policy of increasing dividends each year. The investor may receive more income each year.
3. Greater fool theory. "Investment" for capital gain. The investor

buys a security and hopes it will rise in price and she will be able to sell it in the future at a higher price. There are five main sub-categories of this approach:

(a) Value investing. The price of some stock is $x per share now. The stock's "value" is a financial calculation involving assets, liabilities, income, sales, and other financial facts and future projections. Value investors might buy at $x, believing that its value is $x++ per share. They believe that at some future time, the share price will rise to their calculated value.

(b) Growth investing. The growth rate of some company is a financial calculation involving assets, liabilities, income, sales, and other financial facts and projections. "Growth investors" believe that a company's "growth rate" is so high that its current share price does not yet reflect what it's really worth. They believe that the price of the shares will rise because the company's growth is so strong.

(c) Momentum investing. The price of some security is rising. As long as it keeps rising, the momentum investor wants to own it. (Variations of this theory involve owning stocks with earnings momentum, sales momentum, or momentum in some other aspect of the company's financials.)

(d) Technical investing. These investors track the price and volume of trading in a stock over time. They believe that past price influences future price. They will buy or sell stocks when certain statistical events occur. Often these investors will study market psychology and the price trend of the various industry groups, too.

(e) Look-alike investing. These investors correlate the price movement of one type of investing with another. For example, if the price of crude oil is in an up trend, they may buy shares of oil companies as a way of participating in the up trend of oil itself.

(f) The story stock. The particular sales pitch associated with this stock or industry is so appealing that the story itself creates expanding demand, which in turn causes the stock to rise in price.

These are the three basic theoretical reasons why most investors buy stocks: income, growth of income, and capital gain. The securities industry's analysts and other salesmen turn these reasons into sales pitches.

Suppose we decide to use these kind of ideas to create our own investment techniques. One characteristic of a good investment technique is that it involves us in objectively observing the financial world. And it involves both buying and selling. And it involves testing out our premises. Do you see how even the most simple investment technique protects you from the sales pitches?

BEYOND BASICS

There are other ways that money is made in the stock market that are quite sophisticated. We will list them some of them here. These techniques are worth examining as we gain experience. Here is a partial list:

1. Selling volatility. Investors sell options in order to profit from the decline in time premium over the life of the option.
2. Leveraged buying. Investors buy options in order to speculate on a price change. There is a variation of leveraged buying, where investors use borrowed money to buy certain securities.
3. Hedging. Investors simultaneously buy and sell related securities in hopes of profiting from a change in the difference between their prices.

CAVEAT EMPTOR

There are well-trained salesmen ready to assist us with all the above "ways of making money." Never forget this fact. It's important that our money not be used as cannon fodder for some salesman's commission.

For every honest, hard-working professional in the investment business, there is an incompetent bungler and an amoral crook.

CHAPTER ELEVEN KEY POINTS

- There are two types of stock market participants whose techniques we need to learn: other successful investors and successful con artists.

- There are two reasons why it is important to study the stock market techniques of others:

  (a) All financial techniques have limited life expectancies because of the constantly changing nature of the stockmarket.

  (b) Human beings tend to not want to change once they find something that works. "If it ain't broke, don't fix it." We must be on guard that our human nature may someday cause us to be out of sync with the stock market.

- One source of new investment ideas is the financial press.

- There are three basic ways of making money in the stock market:

  (a) Income investing.

  (b) Growth of income.

  (c) The greater fool theory: buy now and hope to sell later at a higher price.

- The greater fool theory has variations:

  (a) Value investing.

  (b) Growth investing.

  (c) Momentum investing.

  (d) Technical investing, often called "technical trading."

(e) Look-alike investing.

(f) The story stock.

- In addition to basic techniques, there are more complex techniques that should be considered by more experienced investors.
- Another source of ideas about investing is the securities salesman.

chapter twelve

Fifth Key: The Unknown

This chapter introduces our "edge." It takes the healthy scepticism we introduced in chapter one to a new level. It takes the healthy alertness and caution of chapter two to a new level. It takes the objectivity of chapter five to a new level. It gives relevance and purpose to our whole approach to making money in the Tyger's jungle.

WHEN INVESTORS FIRST encounter the five keys, they usually find the fifth the most mysterious.

But as we gain in investment wisdom, the fifth key becomes an increasingly important part of what we do. Eventually it will become the most important of the five keys. And the reason is simple: The fifth key pervades all of the other four.

The reason we need to study ourselves in detail as a lifetime occupation is that there are so many things we don't know about ourselves. It's what we don't know about ourselves that will be our demise.

The reason we need to continually work on perfecting our investment techniques is that it is the unknown weakness of our technique that will cause our loss.

The reason we need to plunge into the real world of investing, to experience the joy and agony of winning and losing, is that financial battle will teach us what we can't know from merely reading a book.

The reason we need to know the enemy's technique is so we can take money from him. (Better if he doesn't know what we're doing.)

OBJECTIVE KNOWLEDGE

Our thesis is that in order to receive a higher rate of return over the long term, we need to become better investors over the long term. We do this by thinking more objectively about investing. This task is very difficult in stock market investing because the stock market is a smoke-and-mirrors world made up of salesmen trying to persuade investors to follow their advice. Their sales pitches always involve some reason to buy or sell some security because it will be more or less valuable in the future than it is now.

Securities analysis is about predicting the future. But the more we understand what it means to be objective, the more we realize that everything in the future is unknown. Nevertheless, the salesman's job is to persuade us that he somehow has knowledge about the future. The salesman believes he knows the unknowable. The investment industry is not objective and they don't want us to be objective either. They want us to believe that they can help us know what can't be known.

FREEDOM

In order to be objective, we have to understand that there are many things we can never know. In order to be free, we have to embrace the unknown.

OUR EDGE

We can never know what the future holds. Our financial opponents don't know what the future holds either. But our financial opponents *think they know.*

This is our edge.

Our techniques are based on studying the past and objectively reacting to current data. Our investment life is experienced in the present with our attention directed toward our pre-determined techniques and toward ourselves. We objectively study what the other participants in the market are thinking and doing.

At no time do we dream about knowing the future. At no time do we bet on the future. At no time do we pretend to know the unknowable.

Acknowledgments

The Roman philosopher Marcus Aurelius said our life is what our thoughts make it. This is particularly true in the world of finance, where our financial success depends on what we think.

I first concieved of this book when I was flying across the Pacific Ocean reading Sogyal Rinpoche's *The Tibetan Book of Living and Dying*. Buddhists teach us that the world is an illusion. Nowhere is this more true than in the world of finance. Thank you, Sogyal Rinpoche.

In addition, my thanks to:

Henry Evering, the Eidetic philosopher, who taught me how to think in two dimensions — then three.

Mervyn Brady, the Irish philosopher and my greatest Teacher, for waking up my soul and putting my life in context. Thank you for teaching me how to love and think at the same time.

Bob Farrell and Dick McCabe, for teaching me technical analysis so early in my carreer.

Robert Prechter and Jack Frost, authors of *The Elliott Wave Principle*.

Robert Edwards and John Magee, for publishing your marvelous book, *Technical Analysis of Stock Trends*, in the year I turned three.

Karl Wagner and Bill Carrigan: You are living proof that this stuff works.

Chris Doyle and Ken Jacobs, my karate senseis, for teaching me to think like a warrior. And to understand the connection between our bodies and our minds, zen and ken.

All the members of the Canadian Society of Technical Analysts, the (US) Market Technicians Association, and the International Federation of Technical Analsysts for making me study this stuff in earnest. Like most stock market endeavors, technical analysis only works when you work at it.

Appendices

APPENDIX ONE: THE THREE Cs OF A BEAR MARKET

IN 1975, WHEN I WAS a rookie stock broker with Merrill Lynch, I discussed the possibility of a bear market with my manager.

"How far down will it go?" I asked.

"Farther than you think," he replied.

These were among the wisest words I heard in those early days.

My manager was telling me that market moves are somehow related to what we think. Later I found out that what *I* thought wasn't really so important. What counted was what the majority of buyers and sellers thought. Still later, I discovered that it wasn't about thinking at all; it was about feeling. What do the majority of buyers and sellers *feel* about the stock market?

I learned that there was a pattern to investors' collective feelings during a bear market. My mentor in those years was the chief market technician at Merrill Lynch, a gentleman named Robert Farrell. Bob taught us the three Cs of a bear market.

He identified three stages of an overall stock market decline: the early, mid, and final stages. He taught that each stage of the decline was accompanied by an overall mood on the part of investors.

COMPLACENCY STAGE

During the early phase of a bear market, investors see that the stock market is falling but don't really mind. They are complacent about the decline. They use words like "correction," "average down," "buy on pull-backs." Their optimism about a continuation of the up trend is so strong that they don't really accept that stock prices are actually going down. Slowly, slowly, they notice that the "corrections" seem to go lower and lower, but the recoveries don't seem to bounce as high. Slowly, their optimism and complacency change.

CONCERNED STAGE

During the mid phase of the bear market, worry sets in. Investors become concerned: "Maybe the economy is worse than we thought." They start to wonder if they should reduce their exposure to the stock market a bit, just in case. They use words like "adjust my asset mix," "keep my powder dry," "maintain a defensive posture." As the market continues its zigzag decline, they may start selling some stocks and perhaps buying defensive stocks. As the deterioration continues, concern accelerates.

CAPITULATION STAGE

In the final stages of a bear market, investors give up on the stock market. Their selling increases dramatically. A type of slow panic sometimes sets in. They start to doubt that stocks are a good investment at all. Maybe they shouldn't own *any* stocks. The market has reached the capitulation stage. They use words like "hit the bid," and "just sell and get me out."

This is a time when investors fire their stockbrokers, sue their financial planners, and read the fine print in their mutual-fund prospectus. The securities industry is plagued by layoffs, branch closures, and downsizing. Volume of trading expands as the decline accelerates. Volatility increases. Often it ends in a selling climax on a day where the volume of trading is exceptionally high. The market opens way lower and somehow struggles back and closes above the opening price. The bear market is over.

Ferrell was not implying that there is a preset script that the stock market must follow during a serious decline. But he accurately observed that the mood of investors changes systematically and sequentially as the market goes down. He also observed that in a bear market, the decline will continue until the capitulation.

APPENDIX TWO: THE FIVE ELLIOTT WAVES OF BULL AND BEAR MARKETS

I SOMETIMES GIVE LECTURES on technical analysis and on Elliott Wave Theory (EWT). This appendix is taken from those lectures. It describes the psychological mood of investors during bull and bear markets.

This is *not* an explanation of EWT. If you are curious, go online and search for Elliott Wave Theory. You will find several good books on this topic. This appendix is for those who may have already read the basics of Ralph Elliott's wave theory and are interested in the concept of investor mood.

Ralph Elliott observed that bull markets unfold in a series of price waves: waves of price increases and decreases. A bull market consists of three up waves, interrupted by two down waves. Bear markets are usually more complex, but the basic building block of the bear market consists of two waves down interrupted by one wave up.

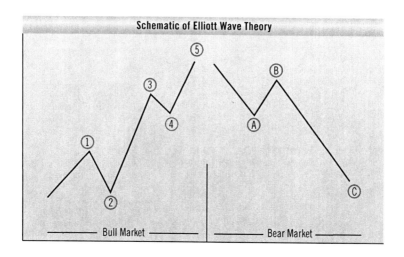

Schematic of Elliott Wave Theory

THE BULL MARKET

Wave 1

Wave 1 begins after a long decline in the stock market. At the end of any bear market, investors are in a terrible mood. Hopelessness, despair, and negativity are everywhere. This is the prevailing mood

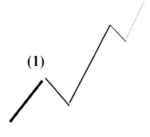

(1)

at the beginning of all bull markets. This is when wave 1 begins. The fact that the market is actually going up is a surprise for investors and is greeted with scepticism. They see it, but don't believe it. Wave 1 is seen as just another short-term blip up in a long-term down trend. The main mood is one of scepticism and disbelief.

Wave 2

Then along comes wave 2, which is often a sharp downward move. "See, I told you this market was going down!" Negativity reasserts itself in this wave. And when wave 2 is over, investors are often even more negative than they were at the market's bottom. This is the clue that helps Elliotticians decide when to buy. There is a divergence between market price and market mood. The mood is more negative than ever, but market prices do not go lower.

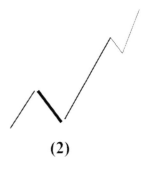

(2)

Wave 3

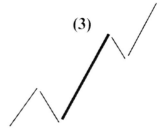

(3)

Wave 3 is where the big money is made. As the upward surge unfolds, the mood of investors' changes from negative to positive. Wave 3 contains the "recognition point," when most investors finally come to accept that the market actually *is* going up. It is normally the longest and strongest of the three up waves in the total five-wave bull market.

Wave 4

Wave 4 seems to come out of no-where. The joy of easy profits is rudely interrupted. Wave 4 tries the patience of investors. "When will the up trend continue?" The over-all mood remains bullish, but a certain impatience may emerge. Investors become less bullish.

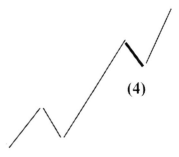

(4)

Wave 5

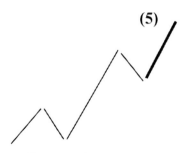

(5)

Wave 5 is the speculative wave in the cycle. Investors go from moderately optimistic to crazy bullish. Many new investors make their entry into the financial markets. Speculation abounds. Initial public offerings often soar to big premiums. Penny stocks come to life! Speculators often borrow money to buy into the fast rising stock market. It is a time of optimism and speculation.

Bull markets change the mood of the investing public from negative and sceptical to positive and optimistic. It happens every time.

THE BEAR MARKET

Wave A

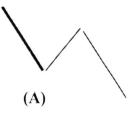

(A)

Because a bear market begins at the end of a long and prosperous bull market, investors are in a positive optimistic mood. Everyone expects to make money. This is the prevailing mood at the beginning of all bear markets. This is when wave A begins. The fact that the market actually went down is a surprise for investors, and is greeted with optimism. Investors see that the market is going down, but do not believe it. Wave A is seen as just another short term correction in a long term up trend. The main mood is optimism and disbelief.

Wave B

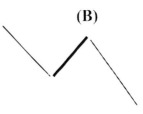

(B)

Then along comes wave B, an upward move. "See, I told you this market was going higher!" Positive investor attitude reasserts itself in this wave. And when wave B is over, investors are often even more positive than they were at the market's top. This is the clue that helps Elliotticians decide when to sell. There is a divergence between market price and market mood. The mood is more positive than ever, but market prices do not go higher.

Wave C

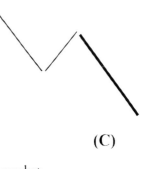

Wave C is where the big money is lost. As the downward surge unfolds, investors' mood changes from positive to negative. It is in this wave that most investors finally come to accept that the market actually *is* going down. It is the longest and strongest of the two

(C)

down waves in the total three-wave bear market.

Caveat emptor: We have deliberately oversimplified EWT in order to illustrate how investor mood changes as the stock market changes. EWT is a complex and beautiful theory that can be very useful. It offers many good investment techniques (second key) to those who are willing to devote their time to it.

OUR LOOK AT THE economic cycle and the stock market cycle earlier in this book showed us how difficult it is to buy the stock market at the bottom and sell at the top. Recall the Countercyclical model from earlier in this book. The worst economic news occurs at the best time to buy stocks. And the best economic news occurs at the worse time to buy stocks. This psychological irony is what makes investing in stocks so difficult.

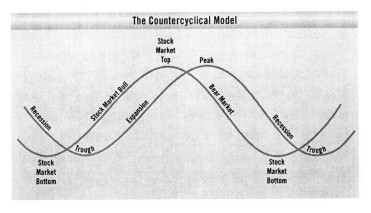

The Countercyclical Model

But there is more to the countercyclical model than market psychology. There is another dimension that can clarify when we should buy in or sell out. This dimension comes from the action of the central banks.

THE GUIDING HAND ...

In modern economies, central banks take action to stabilize the economy. In tough times, they try to stimulate. In times of excess, they try to cool things down. There are a number of ways they achieve their goals. One of the most important is by influencing interest rates.

Interest rates in modern economies reflect two forces: the free market supply and demand for money, and the intention of the central banks. When central banks are cooling down the economies, they do so by increasing interest rates as best they can. When they want to heat up a weak economy, they try to lower interest rates.

We should notice interest rates moving down as economic growth deteriorates and moving up as economic growth accelerates. That would be an indication that the central bank is quietly going about its business of moderating inflation and encouraging steady growth. As the economy changes, central bank interest rate policy will change.

To be more precise, we should notice that, as soon as the economy starts to cool down, central banks will start to lower interest rates. Interest rates are reflected best in the bond market. Bonds go up in price when interest rates go down. So the bond market should start to go up shortly after the economy peaks.

And of course the reverse is true, too. As soon as the economy starts to grow too fast, interest rates should start to go up. The bond market should start to go down.

The following diagram shows the sequence.

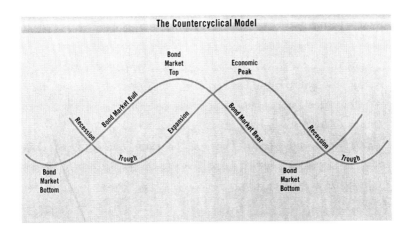

Remember in chapter four how we noted that the stock market leads the economy? Is it correct to say that the economy leads interest rates?

Not really. Central bankers are intelligent, educated people with a mission. Their job is to help their countries maintain stable inflation and stable economic growth. They follow many so-called lead economic indicators and adjust interest rates in trying to head off problems. It's about intention. These important central bankers have economic goals and their actions are intended to serve those goals. They intend to head off economic trouble before it happens. There is no lead-lag relationship between interest rates and the economy until something goes wrong. The only time economic events lead interest rates is when economic problems overcome the actions of the central banks.

MURPHY'S LAW OF ECONOMICS

If something can go wrong it will go wrong. There are two economic things that can go wrong: inflation and economic contraction.

Central bankers try to keep these two forces in balance. But they do not always succeed.

Inflation: If/when an economy heats up too much, inflation is often a problem. Central bankers cool off inflation by raising interest rates. That's why interest rates often start to rise in economic boom times. (Point R-1 on our diagram.)

Economic contraction: If/when the economy cools off too much and starts to shrink, central bankers have to heat it up by lowering interest rates. (Point R-2 on our diagram.)

THE LINK OF LOGIC

Remember the Four Component Model of chapter six? We hypothesized that the intellectual component of the stock market

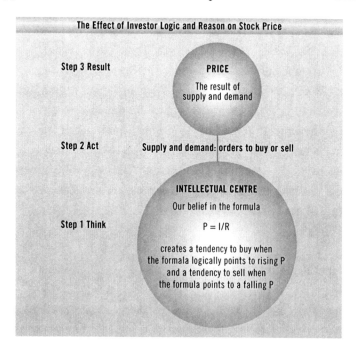

The Effect of Investor Logic and Reason on Stock Price

Step 3 Result — PRICE — The result of supply and demand

Step 2 Act — Supply and demand: orders to buy or sell

Step 1 Think — INTELLECTUAL CENTRE — Our belief in the formula $P = I/R$ creates a tendency to buy when the formala logically points to rising P and a tendency to sell when the formula points to a falling P could be summarized by one grade school formula: Price = Income / Interest Rates.

Is this the link between central bank action and the stock market? Does the bond market lead the stock market?

Let's continue our guided tour of the economy that we began in chapter four.

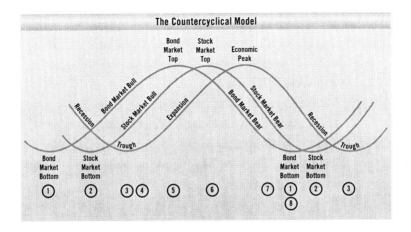

Point 1: The economy is cooling off. The stock market is going down. Investor mood is negative and getting worse. Central banks have over-cooled the economy and decide to try to heat things up again. They try to move interest rates lower. The bond market starts to go up.

Point 2: The economy is still cooling off. Interest rates are still falling. (The bond market is still rising.) Economic news is bad and getting worse. This is the time when the stock market bottoms.

Point 3: The economy is in its darkest hour. There are plant closures, layoffs, bankruptcies ... tough times. Interest rates continue to go lower, and the stock market continues to go higher.

Point 4: At last, the bond market and the stock market are still rising, and the economy is improving. Point 4 is the point of harmony. Everything lines up.

Point 5: As the economy expands, something goes wrong ... Inflation starts to heat up. Central banks reverse their downward pressure on interest rates. The bond market peaks. The stock market and the economy continue up in an atmosphere of rising interest rates.

Point 6: Eventually the stock market peaks and begins to follow the bond market down. The economy is still growing. Inflation is still a problem.

Point 7: The bond market is declining, the stock market is declining, *and* the economy is shrinking. Something has gone wrong!

Point 8: Central banks try to re-heat the economy by lowering interest rates. The bond market starts to rise again. We are back at point 1. Point 8 = point 1.

MURPHY'S LAW REVISITED

Our observation is that central banks operate intentionally, serving specific economic goals. The most important times that they change their policy are when something goes wrong. (Point 5, when inflation heats up too much, and point 8, when the economy cools off too much.)

Question: Does something always go wrong? What happens when things go right? What happens when central banks correctly anticipate and head off inflation? What happens when they correctly anticipate and prevent recession? What happens when they get it right? Does the countercyclical model still work?

Answer #1: Refer to point 5 in our guided tour of the economy. If the central banks successfully cool down inflation by raising interest rates only a little, the bond market may only go down a little, and the stock market may go down only a little. If that happens, the oversimplified smooth lines we have drawn would become zigzagged. Once the zigzag was complete, we would find ourselves back at point 4. The central banks got it right.

Answer #2: Refer to point 6 above. At this point, inflation is still a problem. But when the central banks "get it right" and inflation stays under control, we never get to point 6 — and, by default, we never get to point 7. When they get it right, we stay at points 4 and 5. The bond and stock markets zig and zag higher and higher. Economic growth continues.

GETTING IT RIGHT

Why don't central banks get it right all the time? If recessions can be prevented by central bank policy, why are there still recessions?

HUMAN EMOTION REVISITED

Central bankers have not yet figured out how to control human greed. When they get that right, they will eliminate peace-time recessions. War is another problem: Central bankers' goals change in times of war.

About the Author

Ken Norquay is Director and Chief Market Strategist of CastleMoore Inc., an investment portfolio management company. He is an experienced speaker and writer, having published for many years the creative, informative, and influential newsletter, *The 5-P Report*. He holds the designation of Chartered Market Technician (CMT).

Norquay crafts a defensive investment strategy by combining technical analysis with the mental disciplines and knowledge of human nature provided by the Eastern philosophies. He has a black belt in karate (Nidan). He is a past member of Mervyn Brady's Academy of European Arts and Culture.

He entered the financial services industry in 1975, after serving three years as an army officer. He managed two offices for Merrill Lynch Canada before founding his own investment firm, Market Street Investment House. After selling Market Street, he was a director of Quest Capital Group and established the Glen Nova Division of the Glen Ardith Company. Norquay has also served as a director and president of the Canadian Society of Technical Analysts.